Entrepreneurial Profiles and Behaviour

This book examines the evolution from studying isolated entrepreneurial traits to defining comprehensive entrepreneurial profiles. It explores three innovative profiles—the Human, Harmonic, and *sapiens* entrepreneur—and provides a groundbreaking comparative analysis of their distinctive approaches to entrepreneurial processes and decision-making. This edited collection offers a thorough investigation of how these profiles shape entrepreneurial behaviour, featuring detailed theoretical frameworks, practical applications, and forward-looking perspectives. Readers will gain valuable insights into how these emerging entrepreneurial identities respond to contemporary challenges while preparing for future developments in business and society. The collaborative approach among scholars with different perspectives creates a unique intellectual dialogue that advances entrepreneurship theory.

This volume is essential reading for experienced researchers seeking cutting-edge developments in entrepreneurship studies, early-career academics establishing research trajectories, and graduate students in entrepreneurship, management, and business ethics programmes. It will be of particular interest to those exploring the intersection of entrepreneurial identity, decision-making processes, and sustainable business practices.

Diego Matricano is Associate Professor in the Department of Management at the Università degli Studi della Campania "L. Vanvitelli," Italy.

Mariacarmela Passarelli is Associate Professor in the Department of Management and Law at Università della Calabria, Italy.

Massimiliano Vesci is Professor of Business Management and Entrepreneurship in the Department of Business Sciences at the Unviersità degli Studi di Salerno, Italy.

R.E.Pr.I.S.E - Research on Entrepreneurship Processes, Innovation, and Startup Enterprises
Series Editor: Diego Matricano

Available Titles in this Series:

Entrepreneurial Profiles and Behaviour
Characteristics, Processes, and Decision-Making
Edited by Diego Matricano, Mariacarmela Passarelli, and Massimiliano Vesci

Entrepreneurial Profiles and Behaviour

Characteristics, Processes, and Decision-Making

Edited by
Diego Matricano,
Mariacarmela Passarelli, and
Massimiliano Vesci

Routledge
Taylor & Francis Group
NEW YORK AND LONDON

First published 2026
by Routledge
605 Third Avenue, New York, NY 10158

and by Routledge
4 Park Square, Milton Park, Abingdon, Oxon, OX14 4RN

Routledge is an imprint of the Taylor & Francis Group, an informa business

ISBN: 978-1-041-15787-8 (hbk)
ISBN: 978-1-041-15788-5 (pbk)
ISBN: 978-1-003-68118-2 (ebk)

DOI: 10.4324/9781003681182

Typeset in Times New Roman
by codeMantra

Contents

Contributor biography

Giuseppe Bongiorno is Research Fellow in Management and Entrepreneurship in the Department of Law, Economics and Sociology at the University "Magna Græcia" of Catanzaro.

Preface – rethinking the entrepreneur

From traits to profiles

Entrepreneurship research continues to struggle in answering a deceptively simple question: who is the entrepreneur? For decades, scholars have pursued this question through the systematic identification of individual traits (viz., risk propensity, need for achievement, locus of control, alertness, passion, etc.). While this stream of research has generated an extraordinary body of knowledge, it has also produced a paradox. The more rigorously traits have been examined, the more evident it has become that there is no single clear, stable, agreed on configuration of traits that adequately describes entrepreneurs across contexts, time, and purpose. It is here at this impasse that Diego Matricano, Mariacarmela Passarelli, and Massimiliano Vesci begin this volume.

Rather than attempting to refine, rescue, or further fragment the trait-based tradition, the authors take a different path. More specifically, while they do preserve entrepreneurship's core focus on the individual entrepreneur, they fundamentally reorient the level of analysis. This shift is subtle but consequential, moving from traits to profiles, from disparate attributes to coherent postures, and from static descriptions to ways of being, judging, and acting. Profiles, as developed in this book, are not simply aggregates of traits. Rather, they are higher-order configurations that integrate values, orientations, decision logics, and relationships with context. In doing so, the authors acknowledge that entrepreneurs do not simply possess characteristics; they enact entrepreneurship through patterned behaviours, ethical commitments, and interpretive frameworks that evolve over time and across differing contexts. In this sense, entrepreneurial profiles provide scholars with a pathway to remain grounded in the individual without collapsing entrepreneurship into psychology alone.

Within this framework, this volume is bold in advancing three distinct yet interrelated entrepreneurial profiles: the Humane Entrepreneur, the *Sapiens* Entrepreneur, and the Harmonic Entrepreneur.

Humane entrepreneurs approach entrepreneurship as a strategic posture oriented not only toward innovation and competitiveness but also toward the well-being of people, communities, and the natural environment. Drawing on a relatively new, but growing, body of scholarship, the profile posits entrepreneurs as architects of organizational purpose. Humane entrepreneurs are guided by strategic orientations that put factors such as sustainability and humanistic values into the core of entrepreneurial action rather than treating them as peripheral concerns.

Sapiens entrepreneurs approach entrepreneurship through the lens of wisdom, discernment, and self-mastery. Inspired by classical philosophy (viz., Seneca's notion of sapientia), this profile emphasizes judgement under uncertainty, emotional regulation, and the continuous balancing of competing demands. *Sapiens* entrepreneurs are not defined by moral perfection or heroic foresight, rather they are those driven by an ongoing commitment to learning, reflection, and reasoned action in volatile and ambiguous environments.

Harmonic entrepreneurs advance a relational and integrative view of entrepreneurship, positioning the entrepreneur as an agent who seeks coherence between personal well-being, social responsibility, and care for creation. This profile highlights harmony not as the absence of tension but as the capacity to work constructively through it. By adopting this view, harmonic entrepreneurs reconcile economic objectives with ethical responsibility, innovation with preservation, and individual fulfilment with the collective good.

Importantly, these profiles are not presented as competing ideals or as normative prescriptions for "good" entrepreneurship. Rather, each merely helps to depict the different ways entrepreneurs respond to the growing complexity of contemporary economic and social systems. Collectively, the three do also reflect a shared recognition: that entrepreneurship in the twenty-first century cannot be understood solely through efficiency, opportunity exploitation, or profit maximization, as there are so many other considerations driving contemporary entrepreneurs (cf., meaning, societal impact, harmony, and people).

A closer comparison of these profiles forms the conclusion of this short book, where the authors carefully discuss productive tensions and complementarities between these profiles, culminating in a great platform on which future research can build. Overall, by moving beyond traits towards profiles, the authors invite scholars to rethink how we theorize entrepreneurs, how we study their actions, and how we imagine the future of entrepreneurship research itself.

Eric W. Liguori
Florida State University

1 The entrepreneur

From specific traits to profiles

Giuseppe Bongiorno and Diego Matricano

1.1 Origins of research on entrepreneurial traits

The origins of research on entrepreneurial traits[1] can be traced back to Schumpeter's (1911) contribution. According to the scholar, entrepreneurs must possess specific traits to introduce innovation into the economic system. They must be able to manage risk, possess the ability to exercise leadership, rely on intuition, and be resolute.

Following Schumpeter's contribution, research on entrepreneurial traits consolidates and gains importance with the introduction of the concept of alertness (Kirzner, 1973). This is an individual condition, or status, that allows entrepreneurs to seize market opportunities that others have not yet grasped. Since Kirzner's (1973) contribution, research on entrepreneurial traits has attracted considerable interest among entrepreneurship scholars.

In some cases, this growing interest has led to risks or excesses, consisting in a disproportionate reliance on other fields of research to define the individual traits that entrepreneurs should possess. This is true to the extent that entrepreneurial traits have been examined in the light of anthropology and psychology instead of economics. Unbalanced approaches, such as the trait model (Chell, 1985), have profoundly altered the relationship between entrepreneurship and individual traits. Indeed, research starting from the idea of investigating the typical traits of entrepreneurs has concluded with the hypothesis that entrepreneurship may be a mere projection of an individual's personal traits. This is a rare case, not representative of all studies on the topic. In fact, most scholars have found the right balance between the different research fields, always keeping in mind that the focus of their investigation is the entrepreneur, i.e., an economic agent.

1.2 Developments of research on entrepreneurial traits

To comprehensively systematize research on entrepreneurial traits, it was decided to proceed chronologically and reconstruct their evolution in detail. Four main phases are defined and analysed.

DOI: 10.4324/9781003681182-1

1.2.1 The entrepreneurial traits investigated in the 1950s and 1960s

To begin with, attention is drawn to contributions published between the 1950s and 1960s. During these decades, scholars started to focus on the personal traits that distinguish entrepreneurs from other economic agents (such as capitalists and employees) and from ordinary people (non-entrepreneurs). Scholars focus primarily on the desire for independence (Davids, 1963), a trait that combines the ultimate goal (independence) with action and clearly distinguishes entrepreneurs from non-entrepreneurs, and on the desire for responsibility (Sutton, 1954), understood as the desire to be able to make decisions. From another perspective, they focus on ambition (Davids, 1963), understood as the ability to assert oneself in a social context, self-confidence (Davids, 1963), or communication skills (Pickle, 1964). Indeed, the most widely studied entrepreneurial trait is the need for self-actualization or the need for achievement (McClelland, 1961). This trait consists of the desire to pursue predefined goals in order to achieve success. Despite the theoretical interest it has generated (Begley & Boyd, 1987a, 1987b) and numerous attempts at empirical verification (Johnson, 1990), studies on the need for achievement have produced conflicting results. On the one hand, some scholars emphasize the strong relationship between need for achievement and business success (Shaver & Scott, 1991); on the other, some researchers remark the connection between need for achievement and more cautious entrepreneurial behaviour (Welsh & White, 1981), without ever sacrificing the ultimate goal of success.

All of the traits listed above, reported in Table 1.1, appear to share the same starting point: they aim to explore and explain individuals' initial involvement in entrepreneurship. Scholars' attention has primarily focused on the traits that can drive individuals to become entrepreneurs. This choice appears closely linked to the trend of studies during that historical period. The 1950s and 1960s, in fact, saw the first significant diffusion of entrepreneurial studies, and it is natural that scholars seek to understand and investigate individuals' initial involvement in entrepreneurship.

1.2.2 The entrepreneurial traits investigated in the 1970s and 1980s

Over the next two decades, in the 1970s and 1980s, research on entrepreneurial traits focused on individuals' initial involvement, which is complemented by further studies examining individual traits related to the ability and willingness to compete in the marketplace. Therefore, scholars' attention is now focused on the ability to exercise leadership (Hornaday & Aboud, 1971), the need for power (Winter, 1973), creativity (Timmons, 1978), judgement (Casson, 1982), and the impact that personal motivation can have on corporate growth and performance (Davidsson, 1989). The aforementioned entrepreneurial traits are listed in Table 1.1.

Table 1.1 An overview of the contributions on entrepreneurial traits

Entrepreneurial traits	*Authors*
In the 1950s and 1960s	
Desire for independence	Davids (1963)
Desire for responsibility	Sutton (1954)
Ambition	Davids (1963)
Self-confidence	Davids (1963)
Communication skills	Pickle (1964)
Need for achievement	McClelland (1961)
In the 1970s and 1980s	
Leadership	Hornaday and Aboud (1971)
Entrepreneurial alertness	Kirzner (1973, 1979)
Need for power	Winter (1973)
Creativity	Timmons (1978)
Judgement	Casson (1982)
Personal motivation	Davidsson (1989)
In the 1990s	
Cognitive flexibility	Brugnoli (1990)
Passion for work	Baum (1995)
Self-efficacy	Bandura (1995, 1997)
Resource orchestration	Batstone and Pheby (1996)
Overconfidence	Busenitz and Barney (1997)
'Big Five' model	Goldberg (1993), McCrae and Costa (2008)
Realism/Realistic orientation	Neck et al. (1999)
In the new millennium	
Problem-solving ability	Littunen (2000)
Overconfidence	Simon et al. (2000)
Networking ability	O'Donnell et al. (2001)
Reliability	Stewart and Roth (2001)
Effectiveness	Erikson (2003)
Entrepreneurial optimism	Lowe and Ziedonis (2006)
Emotional intelligence/empathy	Zampetakis et al. (2009)
Entrepreneurial intuition/metacognition	Dane and Pratt (2009)
Divergent thinking/divergent creativity	Ward (2004)
Entrepreneurial passion	Cardon et al. (2013)
Time perspective/future orientation	Valliere (2013)
Resilience/psychological resilience	Ayala and Manzano (2014)
Dopaminergic sensitivity	Nicolaou and Shane (2014)
Dark triad	Klotz and Neubaum (2016)
Grit/perseverance of effort	Mueller et al. (2017)
Neurodiversity traits (e.g., ADHD, dyslexia)	Wiklund et al. (2017)
Emotional self-regulation	De Cock et al. (2020)
Regulatory focus	Lanivich et al. (2025)

Source: Authors' personal elaboration.

1.2.3 The entrepreneurial traits investigated in the 1990s

With the arrival of the 1990s, market competition became increasingly fierce, and at the same time, research on the entrepreneurial traits necessary for competitiveness intensified. Entrepreneurs are now attributed a series of traits, such as flexibility (Brugnoli, 1990), passion for work (Baum, 1995), overconfidence (Busenitz & Barney, 1997), and realism (Neck et al., 1999).

Scholars begin to direct their interest toward different areas of research. On the one hand, they focus on flexibility, passion, and realism. On the other hand, they focus on overconfidence or arrogance. On yet another, various heterogenous traits are combined. The so-called 'Big Five' model (including neuroticism, extraversion, openness to experience, conscientiousness, and agreeableness) theoretically identifies individuals who, depending on their low/high levels of each trait, have different entrepreneurial propensities (Goldberg, 1993; McCrae & Costa, 2008; Zhao & Seibert, 2006). The model does not predict entrepreneurial success, but rather an identikit based on organization, persistence, dedication, intellectual curiosity, being active and assertive, being emotionally stable or unstable, or having a more or less accommodating or ruthless personality (Zhao et al., 2010). These traits anticipate the scenario that characterizes the new millennium. Again, the entrepreneurial traits are reported in Table 1.1.

1.2.4 The entrepreneurial traits investigated in the new millennium

In the new millennium, scholars focus their attention on problem-solving skills (Littunen, 2000), emphasize individual capabilities (Simon et al., 2000), reliability (Stewart & Roth, 2001), effectiveness (Erikson, 2003), optimism (Hmieleski & Baron, 2008; Lowe & Ziedonis, 2006;), and, finally, the ability to interact with others, to network (Greve & Salaff, 2003; O'Donnell et al., 2001). The psychological approach to entrepreneurship replaces the static perspective of trait assessment with a dynamic one, in which traits are interpreted as interconnections that shape cognition, emotions, and motivations for entrepreneurial behaviour. For example, entrepreneurial passion (Cardon et al., 2013; Newman et al., 2021) is considered fundamental to defining the true identity of every entrepreneur, but at the same time, it supports their motivation and perseverance over time in carrying out their activities. At the same time, other contributions emphasize the importance of grit as the ability to maintain consistency and perseverance over the long term, integrating energy and discipline (Mueller et al., 2017). The motivational domain also presents subtle distinctions that tend to characterize a regulatory focus that can be oriented toward exploration or prevention in the pursuit of entrepreneurial goals (Lanivich et al., 2025). In this regard, a key entrepreneurial trait is cognitive flexibility that – based on Brugnoli's contribution (1990) – requires entrepreneurs capable of rapidly and adaptively changing their mental frameworks in turbulent or constantly evolving markets such as digital ones (Dheer & Lenartowicz, 2019;

Furnham & Marks, 2013; Neupane et al., 2025). In some cases, cognitive flexibility recalls resilience, which allows individuals to take advantage of unpleasant situations or failures by transforming them into learning experiences and further energy to pursue entrepreneurial goals (Ayala & Manzano, 2014; Kashdan & Rottenberg, 2010; van Hugten et al., 2021). Therefore, regulating emotions is essential for the psychological survival of entrepreneurs, both for cognitive health and for clear decision-making (Cardon et al., 2012; De Cock et al., 2020).

In recent years, the literature on entrepreneurial traits, considering the cognitive aspects of entrepreneurs, has received increasing attention from more interdisciplinary fields. Building on the work of Kirzner (1973, 2009), Tang et al. (2012) seek to explore entrepreneurial alertness, a cognitive ability characterized by the sensitivity to recognize entrepreneurial opportunities (Chen et al., 2020; Kaish & Gilad, 1991; Kirzner, 1997). These limited cognitive constraints make entrepreneurs more alert to business opportunities and underscore a future-oriented mindset linked to the 'time perspective' trait (Levasseur et al., 2024; Schneider, 2019, 2020; Valliere, 2013). This interest in cognitive aspects also stems from the metacognitive insights and divergent thinking (or divergent creativity) explored by entrepreneurs who demonstrate the ability to find original and useful solutions, along with the ability to make rapid decisions based on learned patterns (Dane & Pratt, 2009; Haynie & Shepherd, 2011; Ward, 2004). At the same time, research on entrepreneurial traits has pushed the boundaries, analysing neurodiversity (ADHD, dyslexia) as cognitive resources capable of promoting exploration, creativity, and rapid response to change (Bongiorno et al., 2025; Hunt et al., 2022; Lerner et al., 2019; Moore et al., 2021; Wiklund et al., 2017). Other contributions have also taken individual biology into account, looking at genetics as the basis for entrepreneurial traits and emphasizing how dopamine can influence exploration, motivation, and entrepreneurial risk (Bönte et al., 2016; Nicolaou & Shane, 2014; Nicolaou et al., 2021; Rietveld et al., 2021). These are joined by socio-affective traits that can outline skills or abilities related to emotional intelligence and empathy (Davis, 2018; Packard & Burnham, 2021; Zampetakis et al., 2009). In fact, understanding, regulating, and using emotions to guide thoughts and actions clarifies how entrepreneurs act and interpret them, combined with a possible understanding of the emotional states of others (Pathak & Muralidharan, 2024; Rhee & White, 2007; Shepherd et al., 2023).

In addition to traits more closely related to 'personality', recent research on the topic considers the so-called 'dark triad' (narcissism, Machiavellianism, and psychopathy). Placed between adaptive and dysfunctional personalities, these are positively evaluated as capable of representing an ambivalent resource depending on the context, level of expression, and the presence of compensatory traits (Brownell et al., 2021; Hmieleski & Lerner, 2016; Klotz & Neubaum, 2016; Kraus et al., 2020). In summary, the entrepreneurial traits mentioned above are listed in Table 1.1.

It is manifest that scholars interested in entrepreneurial traits have produced a vast, complex, fragmented, and multifaceted literature (Kerr et al., 2018). In this context, two traits have remained constant over the decades: risk management and locus of control. For this reason, they must be treated separately.

1.3 The main entrepreneurial traits: risk management and locus of control

1.3.1 Risk management

Among entrepreneurial traits, risk management deserves a separate discussion, as it has perhaps attracted scholarly interest more than any other (Bergner et al., 2023; Martínez-Cañas et al., 2023; Zhao et al., 2021). Already in the earliest definitions proposed (Knight, 1921; Schumpeter, 1911), the entrepreneur is someone who introduces innovations into the economic system and therefore, inevitably, assumes the risks associated with this objective. These definitions seem to characterize the entrepreneurial profile as they attribute to the individual involved an important quality for operating in the marketplace.

Defining what is meant by risk management in the entrepreneurial context, however, is not simple. Over the years, various interpretations have been proposed. One of these is that entrepreneurs must assume all the risks associated with the existing activity. Therefore, they are risk-takers (Churchill, 1997; Welsh & White, 1981). Another interpretation holds that entrepreneurs shouldn't take on all the risk but should be able to tolerate it. In this case, it would be more accurate to describe them as risk-bearing entrepreneurs (Timmons, 1978). According to another view, it is more appropriate to define entrepreneurs as moderate risk-takers (Welsh & White, 1981). In other words, they do not seek to take on high risks, but only moderate risks that can be tolerated. In this sense, it is clear that entrepreneurs seek to take only limited and controllable risks (Churchill, 1997). Alternatively, according to a different interpretation, entrepreneurs evaluate the risk to be taken based on a short- or long-term time horizon (Das & Teng, 1997). From an empirical perspective, tests and measurements of entrepreneurs' risk propensity provide contradictory results. Some studies show that entrepreneurs have a greater propensity for risk than non-entrepreneurs. Other studies, however, find no significant differences between entrepreneurs and non-entrepreneurs on this point. Overall, the strong interest shown by researchers in risk management confirms its relevance, although the heterogeneity of the findings still raises the question of whether this trait applies to all entrepreneurs.

The aforementioned uncertainty has led to two different research paths. The first aimed to delve deeper into the determinants of risk propensity and risk management (Parlich & Bagby, 1995; Weber, 1997; Weber & Hsee, 1999). The second, instead, is interested in examining another entrepreneurial trait, namely tolerance for ambiguity (Budner, 1962; Koh, 1996; McGrath,

1999; Sexton & Bowman, 1985), which also concerns the management of uncertain situations.

Regarding the first line of research, two contributions (Weber, 1997; Weber & Hsee, 1999) are particularly interesting. They highlight and analyse three possible determinants of risk propensity. The first is the perceived risk specific to the desired activity; the second is related to the benefits achievable if the individual decides to undertake that activity; the third and final factor is the individual's personal propensity to take on that specific risk. The decision to focus primarily on the determinants of risk propensity entails a significant shift: the focus shifts from an *ex post* moment, in which the entrepreneur must evaluate whether or not to take on a risk, to an *ex ante* moment, in which the entrepreneur must evaluate whether a risk is truly a risk, that is, whether it is manageable and to what extent. This approach echoes the theory that risk propensity and risk management depend on the interpretation of the context: in this sense, entrepreneurs are characterized by a tendency to interpret unclear and ambiguous economic situations more positively (Parlich & Bagby, 1995). This suggests that it is not the ability to take risks that identifies entrepreneurs, but rather the criteria they use to assess that risk.

The second line of research explores tolerance for ambiguity. Attention now focuses on the behaviour entrepreneurs can adopt in difficult and unpredictable situations (Budner, 1962; Koh, 1996; McGrath, 1999; Sexton & Bowman, 1985). In this case, scholars remain within the same field but narrow their scope. They shift from managing risky situations to managing unexpected situations that could themselves become risky (Koh, 1996; Sexton & Bowman, 1985). Heterogeneity in the definition of risk propensity and management, the theoretical proposal to shift attention to what happens ex ante, and the difficulties in defining tolerance for ambiguity have slowed the progress of studies on the topic. For this reason, the debate on how entrepreneurs distinguish themselves from other economic agents in risky or ambiguous situations remains open.

1.3.2 Locus of control

Locus of control is another entrepreneurial trait that deserves a separate discussion. This concept, originating in social studies (Heider, 1958; Rotter, 1966), consists in feeling capable of controlling the present and determining the future.

In entrepreneurial studies, it is necessary to distinguish between internal and external locus of control. Individuals with an internal locus of control are able to act proactively and, if necessary, modify the context in which they operate to pursue predefined goals. Individual behaviour, therefore, can influence the consequences. Conversely, individuals with an external locus of control are forced to endure what happens in their environment and lack the power or ability to change the situation. In this case, the consequences of human action are influenced by exogenous variables, such as fate or chance. The difference between internal and external locus of control is of great importance as it influences the choices and actions that entrepreneurs intend to undertake. Over the years, several studies have shown that the effects on entrepreneurship are greater and more positive when the locus of control is internal (Cromie, 2000; Koh, 1996; Mueller & Thomas, 2001; Rauch & Frese, 2007a, 2007b).

The concept of locus of control is closely related to two other traits often attributed to entrepreneurs: self-efficacy and self-esteem. The concept of self-efficacy is linked to individuals' perception of themselves or, more precisely, their perception of their own capabilities (Bandura, 1995, 1997). In the field of entrepreneurship, the concept of self-efficacy has attracted considerable interest, and the idea that confidence in one's own abilities positively influences individuals' commitment to entrepreneurship has been widely shared. Indeed, the higher an individual's self-efficacy, the greater the personal capabilities they believe they possess and, consequently, the more challenging the goals they will pursue.

The concept of self-esteem is linked to individuals' evaluation of themselves and their abilities (Rosenberg, 1965). It follows that the higher the self-esteem, the greater the motivation to act. Conversely, the lower the self-esteem, the lower the impulse to act. This suggests that entrepreneurs are typically considered to have high self-esteem.

Empirical findings regarding locus of control, self-efficacy, and self-esteem confirm that these traits are typical of entrepreneurs. However, as scholars themselves frequently emphasize in their commentaries (Cromie 2000; Koh 1996; Mueller & Thomas 2001; Rauch & Frese 2007a, 2007b), any generalizations should be made with due caution, highlighting potential limitations and biases.

1.4 A critical analysis of the findings on specific traits and the shift towards entrepreneurial profiles

As the previous review shows, research on entrepreneurial traits has slowly evolved. Initial contributions, focused on specific traits, have generated a vast, complex, fragmented, and multifaceted literature (Kerr et al., 2018), characterized by a wide range of contradictory definitions (Salmony & Kanbach, 2022; Van Ness & Seifert, 2016). For this reason, scholars have slightly shifted their focus from a list of specific traits (Hayter et al., 2022; Leitch & Harrison, 2016) to a broader view that can combine various individual traits with the entrepreneurial role (Mmbaga et al., 2020; Radu-Lefebvre et al., 2021) without losing sight of the focus on entrepreneurship (Luthans et al., 2015; Nolzen, 2018; Rauch & Frese, 2007a, 2007b; Welter & Scrimpshire, 2021; Zhao et al., 2010).

Following the processual view defined by Shane and Venkataraman (2000) and supported by other contributions (Daspit et al., 2023; Kuratko et al., 2021;

Pidduck et al., 2023), which looks at entrepreneurship as a process that evolves over time in an effort to achieve a final goal, several scholars have proposed going beyond the trait-based approach, calling for a change of perspective (Baron & Shane, 2007; Moroz & Hindle, 2012; Bennett & Chatterji, 2023).

The paradigm of traits as static predictors of success has proven inconsistent, and, already in 1988, Gartner argued that the focus should be shifted to action and process. Entrepreneurship is not a state of being but is defined as dynamic as it develops and evolves over time (Frese & Gielnik, 2014, 2023; Shane & Venkataraman, 2000). In this regard, it is worth recalling the vision of strategic entrepreneurship, proposed by Companys and McMullen (2007), Hitt et al. (2011), and Ireland et al. (2023), and the concepts of causality (planning based on foresight) and effectuation (control of the future based on available means), proposed by Sarasvathy (2001) and Reymen et al. (2015). Despite the approach, the various phases that constitute entrepreneurial processes, although sequential, are dynamic and iterative (Fayolle, 2007; McMullen & Dimov, 2013; Shepherd et al., 2015; Wood et al., 2021). This paradigm shift has led to a perspective that considers the influence of the surrounding environment (Guerrero et al., 2021; Johnsen & Holt, 2023; McMullen & Shepherd, 2006) and its changing conditions (Baron, 2008; Grégoire et al., 2011; Pryor et al., 2016) and the role of teams, networks and/or ecosystems (Chen et al., 2017; de Mol et al., 2015; Renko et al., 2015).

Consequently, more than a single trait is needed to address novel and specific conditions that can reveal when entrepreneurs are acting (Gartner, 1988; Rauch et al., 2009), and the extent of their impact cannot be generalized (Thai & Mai, 2023). This outcome can be compared to the difficult 'muggle hunt' (Kilby, 1971; Ramoglou et al., 2020) and is therefore still the subject of criticism and debate among entrepreneurship scholars (Llewellyn & Wilson, 2003; Salmony & Kanbach, 2022; Thai & Mai, 2023).

1.5 Research framework

The shift anticipated above – from a list of specific traits (Leitch & Harrison, 2016; Hayter et al., 2022) to a broader vision that can combine different individual traits with the entrepreneurial role (Radu-Lefebvre et al., 2021; Mmbaga et al., 2020) – leads to focus on the entrepreneurial profiles that several traits contribute to creating (Denicolai et al., 2015; Espinoza-Benavides & Díaz, 2019). From this perspective, entrepreneurship is no longer seen as a set of possessed traits but as a way of acting, interacting, and constructing content through practices, processes, and contexts (Gregori, 2024; Steyaert, 2007). This is encapsulated in the perspective of entrepreneuring, a verb that describes the act of undertaking and encompasses often overlooked dimensions. The flow of actions describes not only who the entrepreneur is but also what happens in everyday life (Johannisson, 2011; Steyaert & Katz, 2004). A holistic view of entrepreneurial activity is needed, encompassing the features of each entrepreneurial process and analysing the sequence of events and actions, beyond a simple list of personal attributes (Baltar & de Coulon, 2014; Carter et al., 1996; Fayolle, 2007; Frese & Gielnik, 2023; McMullen & Dimov, 2013).

In this way, the concept of entrepreneurial profile, which represents a complex combination of personal attributes, values, experience, actions, context, and strategic choices, offers a multidimensional perspective (Cubico et al., 2010; Denicolai et al., 2015; Van Ness & Seifert, 2015), assumes a noticeable relevance, and develops previous contributions. Obschonka and Stuetzer (2017) propose the Entrepreneurial Personality System model, in which traits are reinterpreted as manifestations of cognitive, affective, and motivational processes that interact in complex ways with the context. Ranfagni and Runfola (2018) also work on the entrepreneurial profiles of the 'businessman' (who focuses on the market and problems to be solved, abandoning passion considered superfluous to business) or the 'artist' (who prioritizes passion at the expense of business performance). The perspective of entrepreneurial profiles also goes beyond the traditional strands linked to 'positive' and 'negative' traits (Salmony & Kanbach, 2022.). In fact, apparently distant conditions can prove to be integrated and capable of promoting new paradigms of inclusion, for example, how cognitive heterogeneity linked to neurodiversity can generate entrepreneurial value (Yu et al., 2021; Bort et al., 2024). Therefore, the goal is not to define an 'ideal personality' that represents all entrepreneurs but to develop a plurality of entrepreneurial profiles, all potentially effective. The following chapters introduce three profiles: the Humane Entrepreneur (Chapter 2), the *Sapiens* Entrepreneur (Chapter 3), and the Harmonic Entrepreneur (Chapter 4).

It is hoped that the profiles proposed below have theoretical implications. They offer a bridge between cognitive, processual, and strategic approaches, emphasizing conceptual advances in the field of entrepreneurship (Denicolai et al., 2015; Frese & Gielnik, 2023). It is no longer a question of 'who has the right traits' but of 'how certain entrepreneurial profiles (with some general characteristics) generate value in a way that is consistent with themselves and the context'. This is a paradigm shift that restores the most authentically human and systemic dimension to entrepreneurial psychology (Bastian et al., 2025; Dileo & García Pereiro, 2019). Therefore, the profiling approach must focus on how engagement in entrepreneurial activity leads to changes at multiple levels, starting with the entrepreneurs themselves (Denicolai et al., 2015; Kuratko et al., 2015; Munoz & Dimov, 2023; Wiklund et al., 2011).

Note

1 In reference to entrepreneurship research, the word 'trait' is different from 'characteristics'. While the former stands for a specific, distinct quality, the latter stands for a broad, general feature. This distinction is important since it reveals two different level of analysis (Amiri & Marimaei, 2012).

References

Amiri, N. S., Marimaei, M. R. (2012). Concept of entrepreneurship and entrepreneurs traits and characteristics. *Scholarly Journal of Business Administration*, *2*(7), 150–155.

Ayala, J. C., Manzano, G. (2014). The resilience of the entrepreneur. Influence on the success of the business. A longitudinal analysis. *Journal of Economic Psychology*, *42*, 126–135.

Baltar, F., de Coulon, S. (2014). Dynamics of the entrepreneurial process: the innovative entrepreneur and the strategic decisions. *Review of Business & Finance Studies*, *5*(1), 69–81.

Bandura, A. (1995). *Self-Efficacy in Changing Societies*. Cambridge University Press, Cambridge, UK.

Bandura, A. (1997). *Self-Efficacy: The Exercise of Control*. Freeman, New York.

Baron, R. A. (2008). The role of affect in the entrepreneurial process. *Academy of Management Review*, *33*(2), 328–340.

Baron, R. A., Shane, S. (2007). Entrepreneurship: a process perspective. In J. R. Baum, M. Frese, R. A. Baron (Eds.), *The Psychology of Entrepreneurship*, 19–40. Psychology Press, New York.

Bastian, B., Hjelle, M., Shepherd, D. (2025). Systemizing entrepreneurial metacognition: thinking about the past and future. *Entrepreneurship Theory and Practice*, 10422587251315664.

Batstone, S., Pheby, J. (1996). Entrepreneurship and decision making: the contribution of GLS Shackle. *International Journal of Entrepreneurial Behavior & Research*, *2*(2), 34–51.

Baum, J. R. (1995). The relation of traits, competencies, motivation, strategy, and structure to venture growth. In W. D. W. D. Bygrave, B. J. Bird, S. Birley, N. C. Churchill, M. G. Hay, R. H. Keeley, J. W. E. Wetzel (Eds.), *Frontiers of Entrepreneurship Research*, 105–117. Babson College, Wellesley, MA.

Begley, T. M., Boyd, D. P. (1987a). A comparison of entrepreneurs and managers of small business firms. *Journal of Management*, *13*(1), 99–108.

Begley, T. M., Boyd, D. P. (1987b). Psychological characteristics associated with performance in entrepreneurial firms and smaller businesses. *Journal of Business Venturing*, *2*(1), 79–93.

Bennett, V. M., Chatterji, A. K. (2023). The entrepreneurial process: evidence from a nationally representative survey. *Strategic Management Journal*, *44*(1), 86–116.

Bergner, S., Auburger, J., Paleczek, D. (2023). The why and the how: a nexus on how opportunity, risk and personality affect entrepreneurial intention. *Journal of Small Business Management*, *61*(6), 2656–2689.

Bongiorno, G., Passarelli, M., Ooms, F., Massaro, S. (2025). The neuroscience of neurodiversity in entrepreneurship. In L. D. Marino, A. C. Corbett, D. A. Lerner (Eds.), *Neurodiversity in Entrepreneurship*, 71–101, chapter 4. Emerald Publishing Limited, Leeds.

Bönte, W., Procher, V. D., Urbig, D. (2016). Biology and selection into entrepreneurship. The relevance of prenatal testosterone exposure. *Entrepreneurship Theory and Practice*, *40*(5), 1121–1148.

Bort, J., Wiklund, J., Crawford, G. C., Lerner, D. A., Hunt, R. A. (2024). The strategic advantage of impulsivity in entrepreneurial action: an agent-based modelling approach. *Entrepreneurship Theory and Practice*, *48*(2), 547–580.

Brownell, K. M., McMullen, J. S., O'Boyle Jr, E. H. (2021). Fatal attraction: a systematic review and research agenda of the dark triad in entrepreneurship. *Journal of Business Venturing, 36*(3), 106106.

Brugnoli, C. (1990). *L'Imprenditorialità per lo Sviluppo di Nuove Aziende*. Egea, Milano.

Budner, S. (1962). Intolerance of ambiguity as a personality variable. *Journal of Personality, 30*(1), 29–50.

Busenitz, L. W., Barney, J. B. (1997). Differences between entrepreneurs and managers in large organizations: biases and heuristics in strategic decision-making. *Journal of Business Venturing, 12*(1), 9–30.

Cardon, M. S., Foo, M. D., Shepherd, D., Wiklund, J. (2012). Exploring the heart: entrepreneurial emotion is a hot topic. *Entrepreneurship Theory and Practice, 36*(1), 1–10.

Cardon, M. S., Gregoire, D. A., Stevens, C. E., Patel, P. C. (2013). Measuring entrepreneurial passion: conceptual foundations and scale validation. *Journal of Business Venturing, 28*(3), 373–396.

Carter, N. M., Gartner, W. B., Reynolds, P. D. (1996). Exploring start-up event sequences. *Journal of Business Venturing, 11*(3), 151–166.

Casson, M. (1982). *The Entrepreneur: An Economic Theory*. Edward Elgar, Northampton, MA.

Chell, E. (1985). The entrepreneurial personality: a few ghosts laid to rest? *International Small Business Journal, 3*(3), 43–54.

Chen, M. H., Chang, Y. Y., Chang, Y. C. (2017). The trinity of entrepreneurial team dynamics: cognition, conflicts and cohesion. *International Journal of Entrepreneurial Behavior & Research, 23*(6), 934–951.

Chen, P. C., Chan, W. C., Hung, S. W., Lin, D. Z. (2020). How entrepreneurs recognise entrepreneurial opportunity and its gaps: a cognitive theory perspective. *Technology Analysis & Strategic Management, 32*(2), 223–238.

Churchill, N. C. (1997). Breaking down the wall: scaling the ladder. In S. Birley, D. Muzyka (Eds.), *Mastering Enterprise*, 61–68. Financial Times/Pitman, London.

Companys, Y. E., McMullen, J. S. (2007). Strategic entrepreneurs at work: the nature, discovery, and exploitation of entrepreneurial opportunities. *Small Business Economics, 28*(4), 301–322.

Cromie, S. (2000). Assessing entrepreneurial inclinations: some approaches and empirical evidence. *European Journal of Work and Organizational Psychology, 9*(1), 7–30.

Cubico, S., Bortolani, E., Favretto, G., Sartori, R. (2010). Describing the entrepreneurial profile: the entrepreneurial aptitude test (TAI). *International Journal of Entrepreneurship and Small Business, 11*(4), 424–435.

Dane, E., Pratt, M. G. (2009). Conceptualizing and measuring intuition: a review of recent trends. In G. P. Hodgkinson, J. K. Ford (Eds.), *International Review of Industrial and Organizational Psychology*, 1–40. Wiley and Blackwell, Chichester, West Sussex.

Das, T. K., Teng, B. S. (1997). Time and entrepreneurial risk behavior. *Entrepreneurship Theory and Practice, 22*(2), 69–88.

Daspit, J. J., Fox, C. J., Findley, S. K. (2023). Entrepreneurial mindset: an integrated definition, a review of current insights, and directions for future research. *Journal of Small Business Management, 61*(1), 12–44.

Davids, L. E. (1963). *Characteristics of Small Business Founders in Texas and Georgia*. Bureau of Business and Economic Research, University of Georgia, Athens, GA.

Davidsson, P. (1989). Entrepreneurship-and after? A study of growth willingness in small firms. *Journal of Business Venturing, 4*(3), 211–226.

Davis, M. H. (2018). *Empathy: A Social Psychological Approach*. Routledge, New York.

De Cock, R., Denoo, L., Clarysse, B. (2020). Surviving the emotional rollercoaster called entrepreneurship: the role of emotion regulation. *Journal of Business Venturing*, *35*(2), 105936.

de Mol, E., Khapova, S. N., Elfring, T. (2015). Entrepreneurial team cognition: a review. *International Journal of Management Reviews*, *17*(2), 232–255.

Denicolai, S., Hagen, B., Pisoni, A. (2015). Be international or be innovative? Be both? The role of the entrepreneurial profile. *Journal of International Entrepreneurship*, *13*(4), 390–417.

Dheer, R. J. S., Lenartowicz, T. (2019). Cognitive flexibility: impact on entrepreneurial intentions. *Journal of Vocational Behavior, 115*, 103339.

Dileo, I., García Pereiro, T. (2019). Assessing the impact of individual and context factors on the entrepreneurial process. A cross-country multilevel approach. *International Entrepreneurship and Management Journal*, *15*(4), 1393–1441.

Erikson, T. (2003). Toward a taxonomy of entrepreneurial learning experiences among potential entrepreneurs. *Journal of Small Business and Enterprise Development*, *10*(1), 106–112.

Espinoza-Benavides, J., Díaz, D. (2019). The entrepreneurial profile after failure. *International Journal of Entrepreneurial Behavior & Research*, *25*(8), 1634–1651.

Fayolle, A. (2007). The dynamic dimension of the entrepreneurial process. In A. Fayolle (Ed.), *Entrepreneurship and New Value Creation: The Dynamic of the Entrepreneurial Process*, 130–145, Cambridge University Press, Cambridge.

Frese, M., Gielnik, M. M. (2014). The psychology of entrepreneurship. *Annual Review of Organizational Psychology and Organizational Behavior, 1*, 413–438.

Frese, M., Gielnik, M. M. (2023). The psychology of entrepreneurship: action and process. *Annual Review of Organizational Psychology and Organizational Behavior*, *10*(1), 137–164.

Furnham, A., Marks, J. (2013). Tolerance of ambiguity: a review of the recent literature. *Psychology*, *4*(09), 717–728.

Gartner, W. B. (1988). “Who is an entrepreneur?” is the wrong question. *American Journal of Small Business*, *12*(4), 11–32.

Goldberg, L. R. (1993). The structure of phenotypic personality traits. *American Psychologist, 48*(1), 26–34.

Grégoire, D. A., Corbett, A. C., McMullen, J. S. (2011). The cognitive perspective in entrepreneurship: an agenda for future research. *Journal of Management Studies*, *48*(6), 1443–1477.

Gregori, P. (2024). Entrepreneuring as provocation and its critical capacity: problematizing and establishing meanings of entrepreneurship. *Entrepreneurship & Regional Development*, *36*(9–10), 1188–1209.

Greve, A., Salaff, J. W. (2003). Social networks and entrepreneurship. *Entrepreneurship Theory and Practice, 28*(1), 1–22.

Guerrero, M., Liñán, F., Cáceres-Carrasco, F. R. (2021). The influence of ecosystems on the entrepreneurship process: a comparison across developed and developing economies. *Small Business Economics*, *57*(4), 1733–1759.

Haynie, J. M., Shepherd, D. (2011). Toward a theory of discontinuous career transition: investigating career transitions necessitated by traumatic life events. *Journal of Applied Psychology*, *96*(3), 501.

Hayter, C. S., Fischer, B., Rasmussen, E. (2022). Becoming an academic entrepreneur: how scientists develop an entrepreneurial identity. *Small Business Economics*, *59*(4), 1469–1487.

Heider, F. (1958). *The Psychology of Interpersonal Relations*. Wiley, Hoboken, NJ.

Hitt, M. A., Ireland, R. D., Sirmon, D. G., Trahms, C. A. (2011). Strategic entrepreneurship: creating value for individuals, organizations, and society. *Academy of Management Perspectives, 25*(2), 57–75.

Hmieleski, K. M., Baron, R. A. (2008). Regulatory focus and new venture performance. *Strategic Entrepreneurship Journal, 2*(4), 285–299.

Hmieleski, K. M., Lerner, D. A. (2016). The dark triad and nascent entrepreneurship: an examination of unproductive versus productive entrepreneurial motives. *Journal of Small Business Management, 54*, 7–32.

Hornaday, J. A., Aboud, J. (1971). Characteristics of successful entrepreneurs. *Personnel Psychology, 24*(2), 141–153.

Hunt, R. A., Lerner, D. A., Johnson, S. L., Sangeeta Badal, Freeman, M. A. (2022). Cracks in the wall: entrepreneurial action theory and the weakening presumption of intended rationality. *Journal of Business Venturing, 37*(3), 106190.

Ireland, R. D., Withers, M. C., Harrison, J. S., Boss, D. S., Scoresby, R. (2023). Strategic entrepreneurship: a review and research agenda. *Entrepreneurship Theory and Practice*, *47*(2), 495–523.

Johannisson, B. (2011). Towards a practice theory of entrepreneuring. *Small Business Economics, 36*(2), 135–150.

Johnsen, C. G., Holt, R. (2023). Narrating the facets of time in entrepreneurial action. *Entrepreneurship Theory and Practice*, *47*(2), 613–627.

Johnson, B. R. (1990). Toward a multidimensional model of entrepreneurship. *Entrepreneurship Theory and Practice, 14*(3), 39–54.

Kaish, S., Gilad, B. (1991). Characteristics of opportunities search of entrepreneurs versus executives – sources, interests, general alertness. *Journal of Business Venturing, 6*(1), 45–61.

Kashdan, T. B., Rottenberg, J. (2010). Psychological flexibility as a fundamental aspect of health. *Clinical Psychology Review*, *30*(7), 865–878.

Kerr, S. P., Kerr, W. R., Xu, T. (2018). Personality traits of entrepreneurs: a review of recent literature. *Foundations and Trends® in Entrepreneurship*, *14*(3), 279–356.

Kilby, P. (1971). *Entrepreneurship and Economic Development*. Free Press, New York.

Kirzner, I. M. (1973). *Competition and Entrepreneurship*. University of Chicago Press, Chicago, IL.

Kirzner, I. M. (1979). *Perception, Opportunity and Profit*. University of Chicago Press, Chicago, IL.

Kirzner, I. M. (1997). Entrepreneurial discovery and the competitive market process: an Austrian approach. *Journal of Economic Literature, 35*(1), 60–85.

Kirzner, I. M. (2009). The alert and creative entrepreneur: a clarification. *Small Business Economics, 32*(2), 145–152.

Klotz, A. C., Neubaum, D. O. (2016). Article commentary: research on the dark side of personality traits in entrepreneurship: observations from an organizational behavior perspective. *Entrepreneurship Theory and Practice*, *40*(1), 7–17.

Knight, F. H. (1921). *Risk, Uncertainty and Profit*. Houghton Mifflin, Iowa City, IA.

Koh, H. C. (1996). Testing hypotheses of entrepreneurial characteristics: a study of Hong Kong MBA students. *Journal of Managerial Psychology, 11*(3), 12–25.

Kraus, S., Traunmüller, V., Kailer, N., Tiberius, V. (2020). The dark triad in entrepreneurship research—a systematic literature review. *Journal of Enterprising Culture, 28*(04), 353–373.

Kuratko, D. F., Fisher, G., Audretsch, D. B. (2021). Unravelling the entrepreneurial mindset. *Small Business Economics*, *57*(4), 1681–1691.

Kuratko, D. F., Morris, M. H., Schindehutte, M. (2015). Understanding the dynamics of entrepreneurship through framework approaches. *Small Business Economics*, *45*(1), 1–13.

Lanivich, S. E., Adomako, S., Vardaman, J. M., Donbesuur, F., Tang, J. (2025). Founder regulatory focus: effects on entrepreneurial orientation and venture performance. *Strategic Entrepreneurship Journal, 19*(3), 481–507.

Leitch, C. M., Harrison, R. T. (2016). Identity, identity formation and identity work in entrepreneurship: conceptual developments and empirical applications. *Entrepreneurship & Regional Development*, *28*(3–4), 177–190.

Lerner, D. A., Verheul, I., Thurik, R. (2019). Entrepreneurship and attention deficit/hyperactivity disorder: a large-scale study involving the clinical condition of ADHD. *Small Business Economics, 53*, 381–392.

Levasseur, L., Lanivich, S. E., Kalubandi, S. C., Sanaria, A. (2024). Time perspective and entrepreneurs' alertness. *Entrepreneurship Theory and Practice*, 10422587241241823.

Littunen, H. (2000). Entrepreneurship and the characteristics of the entrepreneurial personality. *International Journal of Entrepreneurial Behavior & Research, 6*(6), 295–310.

Llewellyn, D. J., Wilson, K. M. (2003). The controversial role of personality traits in entrepreneurial psychology. *Education + Training*, *45*(6), 341–345.

Lowe, R. A., Ziedonis, A. A. (2006). Overoptimism and the performance of entrepreneurial firms. *Management Science, 52*(2), 173–186.

Luthans, F., Youssef-Morgan, C. M., Avolio, B. J. (2015). *Psychological Capital and Beyond*. Oxford University Press, Oxford.

Martínez-Cañas, R., Ruiz-Palomino, P., Jiménez-Moreno, J. J., Linuesa-Langreo, J. (2023). Push versus pull motivations in entrepreneurial intention. *European Research on Management and Business Economics, 29*(2), 100214.

McClelland, D. C. (1961). *The Achieving Society*. Van Nostrand, New York.

McCrae, R. R., Costa, P. T. Jr (2008). The five-factor theory of personality. In O. P. John, R. W. Robins, L. A. Pervin (Eds.), *Handbook of Personality: Theory and Research*, 159–181. The Guilford Press, New York.

McGrath, R. G. (1999). Falling forward: real options reasoning and entrepreneurial failure. *Academy of Management Review, 24*(1), 13–30.

McMullen, J. S., Dimov, D. (2013). Time and the entrepreneurial journey: the problems and promise of studying entrepreneurship as a process. *Journal of Management Studies, 50*(8), 1481–1512.

McMullen, J. S., Shepherd, D. A. (2006). Entrepreneurial action and the role of uncertainty in the theory of the entrepreneur. *The Academy of Management Review, 31*(1), 132–152.

Mmbaga, N. A., Mathias, B. D., Williams, D. W., Cardon, M. S. (2020). A review of and future agenda for research on identity in entrepreneurship. *Journal of Business Venturing*, *35*(6), 106049.

Moore, C. B., McIntyre, N. H., Lanivich, S. E. (2021). ADHD-related neurodiversity and the entrepreneurial mindset. *Entrepreneurship Theory and Practice, 45*(1), 64–91.

Moroz, P. W., Hindle, K. (2012). Entrepreneurship as a process: toward harmonizing multiple perspectives. *Entrepreneurship Theory and Practice*, *36*(4), 781–818.

Mueller, B. A., Wolfe, M. T., Syed, I. (2017). Passion and grit: an exploration of the pathways leading to venture success. *Journal of Business Venturing*, *32*(3), 260–279.

Mueller, S. L., Thomas, A. S. (2001). Culture and entrepreneurial potential: a nine-country study. *Journal of Business Venturing, 16*(1), 51–75.

Munoz, P., Dimov, D. (2023). Facing the future through entrepreneurship theory: a prospective inquiry framework. *Journal of Business Venturing, 38*(4), 106303.

Neck, C. P., Neck, H. M., Manz, C. C., Godwin, J. (1999). "I think I can; I think I can": a self-leadership perspective. *Journal of Managerial Psychology, 14*(6), 477–501.

Neupane, S. M., Bhattarai, P. C., Lowery, C. L. (2025). Personality traits in describing entrepreneurial intentions: a sequential mixed methods study. *Journal of Innovation and Entrepreneurship, 14*(50), 1–35.

Newman, A., Obschonka, M., Moeller, J., Chandan, G. G. (2021). Entrepreneurial passion: a review, synthesis, and agenda for future research. *Applied Psychology, 70*(2), 816–860.

Nicolaou, N., Phan, P. H., Stephan, U. (2021). The biological perspective in entrepreneurship research. *Entrepreneurship Theory and Practice, 45*(1), 3–17.

Nicolaou, N., Shane, S. (2014). Biology, neuroscience, and entrepreneurship. *Journal of Management Inquiry, 23*(1), 98–100.

Nolzen, N. (2018). The concept of psychological capital: a comprehensive review. *Management Review Quarterly, 68*(3), 237–277.

Obschonka, M., Stuetzer, M. (2017). Integrating psychological approaches to entrepreneurship: the entrepreneurial personality system (EPS). *Small Business Economics, 49*(1), 203–231.

O'Donnell, A., Gilmore, A., Cummins, D., Carson, D. (2001). The network construct in entrepreneurship research: a review and critique. *Management Decision, 39*(9), 749–760.

Packard, M. D., Burnham, T. A. (2021). Do we understand each other? Toward a simulated empathy theory for entrepreneurship. *Journal of Business Venturing, 36*(1), 106076.

Parlich, L., Bagby, D. (1995). Using cognitive theory to explain entrepreneurial risk-taking. *Journal of Business Venturing, 10*(6), 425–438.

Pathak, S., Muralidharan, E. (2024). Contextualizing emotional intelligence for commercial and social entrepreneurship. *Small Business Economics, 62*(2), 667–686.

Pickle, H. B. (1964). *Personality and Success: An Evaluation of Personal Characteristics of Successful Small Business Managers*. Small Business Research Series No. 4, U.S. Government Printing Office, Washington, DC.

Pidduck, R. J., Clark, D. R., Lumpkin, G. T. (2023). Entrepreneurial mindset: dispositional beliefs, opportunity beliefs, and entrepreneurial behavior. *Journal of Small Business Management, 61*(1), 45–79.

Pryor, C., Webb, J. W., Ireland, R. D., Ketchen, Jr, D. J. (2016). Toward an integration of the behavioral and cognitive influences on the entrepreneurship process. *Strategic Entrepreneurship Journal, 10*(1), 21–42.

Radu-Lefebvre, M., Lefebvre, V., Crosina, E., Hytti, U. (2021). Entrepreneurial identity: a review and research agenda. *Entrepreneurship Theory and Practice*, *45*(6), 1550–1590.

Ramoglou, S., Gartner, W. B., Tsang, E. W. (2020). "Who is an entrepreneur?" is (still) the wrong question. *Journal of Business Venturing Insights*, *13*, e00168.

Ranfagni, S., Runfola, A. (2018). Connecting passion: distinctive features from emerging entrepreneurial profiles. *Journal of Business Research, 92*, 403–411.

Rauch, A., Frese, M. (2007a). Born to be an entrepreneur? Revisiting the personality approach to entrepreneurship. *Journal of Applied Psychology, 92*(1), 93–112.

Rauch, A., Frese, M. (2007b). Let's put the person back into entrepreneurship research: a meta-analysis on the relationship between business owners' personality traits, business creation, and success. *European Journal of Work and Organizational Psychology, 16*(4), 353–385.

Rauch, A., Wiklund, J., Lumpkin, G. T., Frese, M. (2009). Entrepreneurial orientation and business performance: an assessment of past research and suggestions for the future. *Entrepreneurship Theory and Practice, 33*(3), 761–787.

Renko, M., El Tarabishy, A., Carsrud, A. L., Brännback, M. (2015). Understanding and measuring entrepreneurial leadership style. *Journal of Small Business Management, 53*(1), 54–74.

Reymen, I. M., Andries, P., Berends, H., Mauer, R., Stephan, U., Van Burg, E. (2015). Understanding dynamics of strategic decision making in venture creation: a process study of effectuation and causation. *Strategic Entrepreneurship Journal, 9*(4), 351–379.

Rhee, K. S., White, R. J. (2007). The emotional intelligence of entrepreneurs. *Journal of Small Business & Entrepreneurship, 20*(4), 409–425.

Rietveld, C. A., Slob, E. A., Thurik, A. R. (2021). A decade of research on the genetics of entrepreneurship: a review and view ahead. *Small Business Economics, 57*(3), 1303–1317.

Rosenberg, M. (1965). *Society and the Adolescent Self-Image*. Princeton University Press, Princeton, NJ.

Rotter, J. B. (1966). Generalized expectancies for internal versus external control of reinforcement. *Psychological Monographs, 80*(1), 1-28.

Salmony, F. U., Kanbach, D. K. (2022). Personality trait differences across types of entrepreneurs: a systematic literature review. *Review of Managerial Science, 16*(3), 713–749.

Sarasvathy, S. D. (2001). Causation and effectuation: toward a theoretical shift from economic inevitability to entrepreneurial contingency. *Academy of Management Review, 26*(2), 243–263.

Schneider, D. W. (2019). Alertness and cognitive control: is there a spatial attention constraint? *Attention, Perception, & Psychophysics, 81*, 119–136.

Schneider, D. W. (2020). Alertness and cognitive control: interactions in the spatial Stroop task. *Attention, Perception, & Psychophysics, 82*, 2257–2270.

Schumpeter, J. A. (1911). *The Theory of Economic Development: An Inquiry into Profits, Capital, Credit, Interest and Business Cycle*, 1934 edition. Harvard University Press, Cambridge, MA.

Sexton, D. L., Bowman, N. B. (1985). The entrepreneur: a capable executive and more. *Journal of Business Venturing, 1*(1), 129–140.

Shane, S., Venkataraman, S. (2000). The promise of entrepreneurship as a field of research. *Academy of Management Review, 25*(1), 217–226.

Shaver, K. G., Scott, L. R. (1991). Person, process, choice: the psychology of new venture creation. *Entrepreneurship Theory and Practice, 16*(2), 23–45.

Shepherd, D. A., Seyb, S., Williams, T. A. (2023). Empathy-driven entrepreneurial action: well-being outcomes for entrepreneurs and target beneficiaries. *Journal of Business Venturing, 38*(2), 106290.

Shepherd, D. A., Williams, T. A., Patzelt, H. (2015). Thinking about entrepreneurial decision making: review and research agenda. *Journal of Management, 41*(1), 11–46.

Simon, M., Houghton, S. M., Aquino, K. (2000). Cognitive biases and risk perception. *Journal of Business Venturing, 15*(2), 113–134.

Stewart, W. H., Roth, P. L. (2001). Risk propensity differences between entrepreneurs and managers. *Journal of Applied Psychology, 86*(1), 145–153.

Steyaert, C. (2007). 'Entrepreneuring' as a conceptual attractor? A review of process theories in 20 years of entrepreneurship studies. *Entrepreneurship and Regional Development, 19*(6), 453–477.

Steyaert, C., Katz, J. (2004). Reclaiming the space of entrepreneurship in society: geographical, discursive and social dimensions. *Entrepreneurship & Regional Development, 16*(3), 179–196.

Sutton, F. X. (1954). *Entrepreneurship and Economic Growth.* Harvard University Press, Cambridge, MA.

Tang, J., Kacmar, K. M. M., Busenitz, L. (2012). Entrepreneurial alertness in the pursuit of new opportunities. *Journal of Business Venturing, 27*(1), 77–94.

Thai, Q. H., Mai, K. N. (2023). Entrepreneurial traits: a systematic literature review. *Management Review Quarterly, 74*, 1–69.

Timmons, J. A. (1978). *New Venture Creation: A Guide to Entrepreneurship.* Irwin, Toronto.

Valliere, D. (2013). Towards a schematic theory of entrepreneurial alertness. *Journal of Business Venturing, 28*(3), 430–442.

van Hugten, J., el Hejazi, Z. N., Brassey, J., Vanderstraeten, J., Cannaerts, N., Loots, E., Coreynen, W., van Witteloostuijn, A. (2021). What makes entrepreneurs happy? Psychological flexibility and entrepreneurs' satisfaction. *Journal of Business Venturing Insights, 16*, e00263.

Van Ness, R. K., Seifert, C. F. (2016). A theoretical analysis of the role of characteristics in entrepreneurial propensity. *Strategic Entrepreneurship Journal, 10*(1), 89–96.

Ward, T. B. (2004). Cognition, creativity, and entrepreneurship. *Journal of Business Venturing, 19*(2), 173–188.

Weber, E. U., Hsee, C. (1999). Models of decision making. *Journal of Risk and Uncertainty, 19*(1–3), 7–42.

Weber, M. (1997). *Economy and Society*. University of California Press, Oakland, CA.

Welsh, J. A., White, J. F. (1981). A small business is not a little big business. *Harvard Business Review, 59*(4), 18–27.

Welter, C., Scrimpshire, A. (2021). The missing capital: the case for psychological capital in entrepreneurship research. *Journal of Business Venturing Insights, 16*, e00267.

Wiklund, J., Davidsson, P., Audretsch, D. B., Karlsson, C. (2011). The future of entrepreneurship research. *Entrepreneurship Theory and Practice, 35*(1), 1–9.

Wiklund, J., Yu, W., Tucker, R., Marino, L. D. (2017). ADHD, impulsivity and entrepreneurship. *Journal of Business Venturing, 32*(6), 627–656.

Winter, D. G. (1973). *The Power Motive*. Free Press, New York.

Wood, M. S., Bakker, R. M., Fisher, G. (2021). Back to the future: a time-calibrated theory of entrepreneurial action. *Academy of Management Review, 46*(1), 147–171.

Yu, W., Wiklund, J., Pérez-Luño, A. (2021). ADHD symptoms, entrepreneurial orientation (EO), and firm performance. *Entrepreneurship Theory and Practice, 45*(1), 92–117.

Zampetakis, L. A., Kafetsios, K., Bouranta, N., Dewett, T., Moustakis, V. S. (2009). On the relationship between emotional intelligence and entrepreneurial attitudes and intentions. *International Journal of Entrepreneurial Behavior & Research, 15*(6), 595–618.

Zhao, H., Seibert, S. E. (2006). The big five personality dimensions and entrepreneurial status: a meta-analytical review. *Journal of Applied Psychology, 91*(2), 259–271.

Zhao, H., Seibert, S. E., Lumpkin, G. T. (2010). The relationship of personality to entrepreneurial intentions and performance: a meta-analytic review. *Journal of Management, 36*(2), 381–404.

Zhao, W., Yang, T., Hughes, K. D., Li, Y. (2021). Entrepreneurial alertness and business model innovation. *International Entrepreneurship and Management Journal, 17*(2), 839–864.

2 The Humane Entrepreneur

Massimiliano Vesci

2.1 Introduction: how the concept was conceived

Entrepreneurs have been historically connected with a number of traits or characteristics such as alertness (Kirzner, 1979, 1973) in searching for new entrepreneurial opportunities (Shane & Venkataraman, 2000), risk-taking (Covin & Slevin, 1989), creativity and caring for innovation (Schumpeter, 1934), entrepreneurial self-efficacy (Chen et al., 1998), etc., just to cite some discussed in the entrepreneurship field. The prevailing role of the traditional economic theory (Baumol, 1968, 1990, 1994) has habitually assumed that entrepreneurs, contributing to economic system development, are driven essentially by personal opportunistic behaviour. Although this is true and although it is true that entrepreneurs still engage in opportunistic behaviour for profit maximization, it is also absolutely true that this perspective has often limited or even overlooked the possibility to investigate if and how entrepreneurs in their decision-making combine financial goals and opportunistic behaviour with broader objectives that are important for other key players within the business, such as employees, the local community, and the environment, thus expanding the strategic posture of the firm.

However, in the last decades significant transformations occurred and a meaningful shift in understanding can be pointed out. First, economic system with its recurring crisis and various discontinuity points in competitive landscape has demonstrated that its balanced development cannot be associated only with few entrepreneurial drivers (e.g., opportunistic behaviour, market equilibrium, etc.). Nowadays, entrepreneurs have to scan a plethora of circumstances, values, stakeholders, etc. More clearly, entrepreneurs driven only by opportunism and neglecting to weigh up key players like employees, communities, and environment, in defining firm's strategy and business model, are often not in line with certain types of new competitive scenarios. Second, there is now a widespread recognition that entrepreneurs can influence not just economic growth and customers' behaviour but also environmental sustainability, local communities, and employees' well-being. Paying attention to different stakeholders (e.g., employees, local communities, etc.) with a precise

DOI: 10.4324/9781003681182-2

strategic posture and an expansion of the purpose of corporations is no longer a matter of isolated, nevertheless illuminated, and the Humane Entrepreneurs as in the past (e.g., Adriano Olivetti in the 1960s of last century) but is a question that the realm of real business is trying to answer. From one side the 2019 Business Roundtable's (2019) "Statement on the Purpose of a Corporation" established new standards for entrepreneurship through its focus on generating value for not only shareholders, customers, suppliers, and communities but also employees, especially in terms of quality job conditions. From another side, the corporate world is showing many firms that, being sensitive to the aforementioned calls and concerns, have implemented successful business models that strategically aim to achieve sustainability goals and cultivate healthy workplace dynamics. For example, Brunello Cucinelli, a prominent figure in the fashion and luxury industry, is recognized for infusing concepts from past Western humanism into the foundation of his business strategy. Similarly, Loccioni, a family-run business that is a global leader in the design and production of automation and quality control systems for home appliances and components, has a clear strategic stance that prioritizes people and their personal development while also honouring the environment. Third, after decades of theories focused on stakeholder assessment, corporate social responsibility, and caring for environmental concerns never clearly aimed at describing an entrepreneurial strategic posture and often implicitly inspired by strategic management perspective, new trends among entrepreneurship's scholars have arisen. Humane Entrepreneurship – HumEnt (Kim et al., 2018; Parente et al., 2018), emerged as an innovative approach that identifies an entrepreneurial strategic posture able to address these global challenges, integrating sustainability and human-resource attention as crucial firm strategic posture.

Assuming the perspective of Upper Echelon Theory (Hambrick & Mason, 1984), corporations are mirrored image of entrepreneurs and managers. Thus, corporations' strategic choices depend on the entrepreneurs' and managers' profile. For this reason, this chapter, building on HumEnt, identifies the Humane Entrepreneur as an individual (better, entrepreneurial profile) who emphasizes the development and implementation of innovative business models pursuing the natural environment, having the aim to enhance the quality of life within the local community by addressing significant social values and pressing issues. Additionally, such an entrepreneur seeks to foster greater employee engagement and empowerment by adopting approaches rooted in humanistic principles (Melé, 2003). The Humane Entrepreneur is not "the entrepreneur" for "all seasons" and for "all enterprise" because it is shaped from specific external, internal, and individual factors such as certain types of competitive context, societal pressure, organizational culture, personal beliefs, and credos (Parente et al., 2018; Vesci et al., 2025) that clearly differ depending on business, company, and environment condition, having in any case a clear and strong financial goal.

The remainder of the chapter is arranged as follows. First, HumEnt theoretical framework is described. Building upon the concept of Entrepreneurial Orientation (EO), as established by Covin and Slevin (1989), which serves as foundational entrepreneurial strategic posture of HumEnt, then the entrepreneur's strategic behaviour is examined. Emphasis is placed on entrepreneur's commitment to sustainability, encompassing both environmental and social dimensions, as well as entrepreneur's strategic efforts in ensuring the well-being of the company's global workforce (Kim et al., 2018). Finally, Humane Entrepreneur characteristics and their impact on decision-making are analysed. The chapter concludes tracing future research's trajectories.

2.2 The origin of HumEnt and HEO

The HumEnt theory (Botti & Parente, 2024; Kim et al., 2018; Parente & Kim, 2021; Parente et al., 2018, 2021; Vesci et al., 2023, 2024) was developed to describe and possibly delineate a specific entrepreneurial strategic posture in contemporary business landscape. More precisely, if the twentieth century has witnessed the emergence of entrepreneurial firms (Covin & Slevin, 1989) that demonstrate a distinct entrepreneurial strategic orientation differing from the conservative one, the context of the twenty-first century is pushing some entrepreneurs towards an enlargement of their basic (entrepreneurial) strategic posture represented, integrating sustainability initiatives, optimizing employee engagement and empowerment, and actively sustaining the betterment of the local community.

From this perspective, HumEnt (Parente et al., 2018; Vesci et al., 2023, 2024) developed a crucial construct (namely, Humane Entrepreneurial Orientation, HEO) for analysing these novel entrepreneurial strategic configurations. These configurations have materialized in response to increasing demands from political entities, industry associations, and the broader societal domain (e.g., Business Roundtable, 2019; United Nations, 2015). These external forces demand the adoption of elevated standards for corporate responsibility, specifically concerning stakeholder-centric values directed toward employees, local communities, and the environment.

The central construct within the HumEnt theory is the Humane Entrepreneurial Orientation – HEO (Parente et al., 2021; Vesci et al., 2023), which represents an enlarged entrepreneurial strategic posture. Although, within the theoretical domain of HumEnt, HEO has been subject to dual conceptualizations in the extant literature (Kim et al., 2018; Parente et al., 2018), embracing Parente et al. (2018) approach, specifically, HEO reflects: "the extent to which entrepreneurs and top managers are inclined to take care of a firm's competitiveness, to take care of their human resources and to take care of relevant social values and concerns, including those regarding environmental sustainability" (Parente et al., 2021, p. 512).

Following this definition and considering that HumEnt refers to organizations that exhibit an entrepreneurial nature consistent with Covin and Slevin (1989) and that also adopt a strategic posture oriented toward sustainability, workforce engagement and enablement, and local community enhancement, the focal HEO dimension should accordingly encompass all the aforementioned components. This alignment ensures that HEO accurately captures the full scope of this novel, integrated strategic posture.

More clearly, HEO is conceptualized as an expanded entrepreneurial strategic posture, integrating the foundational EO (Covin & Lumpkin, 2011; Covin & Slevin, 1989, 1990, 1991) with the additional components of sustainability-oriented behaviour and caring for humane-resource. Specifically, HEO incorporates the following three strategic dimensions:

- Entrepreneurial Orientation (EO) (Covin & Slevin, 1989): it serves as the baseline dimension, quantifying the degree to which an organization exhibits an entrepreneurial versus a conservative strategic posture.
- Sustainability Orientation (SO): it represents a firm-level strategic orientation characterized by both strong commitment to environmental preservation and to society-driven initiatives and actions aimed at improving the quality of life within the local community (Parente et al., 2021).
- Human-Resource Orientation (HRO): it refers to the strategic behaviours and deliberate actions an organization undertakes to achieve superior employee engagement and enablement through humanistic approaches and modalities (Kim et al., 2018, 2021; Vesci et al., 2025). This dimension focuses on the internal human capital management strategy.

2.2.1 EO: the needed core to have entrepreneurship

Shifting the focus from individual psychology to actions, Covin and Slevin (1991) advanced a crucial conceptual refinement in advancing entrepreneurship theories. They argued for a behavioural model of entrepreneurship, positing that the entrepreneurial process is fundamentally defined by observable actions rather than by internal psychological profiles or static personal attributes. As Covin and Slevin (1991, p. 8) state, "A behavioral model of entrepreneurship is suggested because behaviors rather than attributes are what give meaning to entrepreneurial process… we know entrepreneurs through their actions". Consistent with this behavioural emphasis, Covin and Slevin (1990, p. 125) defined strategic posture as a firm's "overall competitive orientation", positioning this organization's strategic posture along a continuum anchored by two extremes (Covin & Slevin, 1989). At one end lies the conservative strategic posture, typified through absence of innovation, absolute avoidance of risk, and lack of proactive change. At the opposite end is the entrepreneurial strategic posture, which is defined by high levels of innovativeness, risk-taking, and proactiveness.

In their analysis of firm competitive behaviour, Covin and Slevin (1989) demonstrated the strategic benefits of the entrepreneurial posture, particularly for small firms operating in hostile environments (those with intense competition and fewer inherent opportunities). They noted that an aggressive entrepreneurial approach, built upon proactive, innovative, and risk-taking efforts, is more effective in gaining or sustaining a competitive advantage than a passive, reactive, or conservative strategy (Covin & Slevin, 1989).

This foundational work on strategic posture established a productive stream of research and formalized the EO (Covin & Slevin, 1989) as the key theoretical construct used to operationalize and measure a firm's entrepreneurial strategic behaviour.

Consequently, within the HEO, EO as above delineated constitutes inevitably the core of the construct, being HEO undoubtedly an entrepreneurship's dimension. Having embraced the behavioural approach proposed by Covin and Slevin (1991), the starting point can only be that of EO (Parente et al., 2018; Vesci et al., 2024).

2.2.2 SO: caring for environment and community

The second pillar on which the HumEnt strategic behaviour is built on is expressed by SO. Literature delineates three distinct research trajectories concerning the conceptualization of sustainability (Belz & Binder, 2017; Schaltegger & Wagner, 2011; Shepherd & Patzelt, 2011). Initially, research efforts have been largely concentrated on exploring the environmental aspects of sustainability. Studies in this early predominant wave of investigation (Linnanen, 2002; O'Neill & Gibbs, 2016) characterized ventures based on their capacity to achieve environmental goals and incorporate ecological principles into their operations. A second stream of studies subsequently emerged, documenting the social aspects of sustainability. These scholarly works (De Clercq & Voronov, 2011; Lumpkin et al., 2013; Zahra et al., 2009) explained sustainability in terms of a venture's commitment to addressing social requirements and contributing to the improvement of social wealth. More recently, particularly over the last decade, a comprehensive or holistic approach to sustainable entrepreneurship has become firmly established in the literature. This trajectory encompasses studies (Schaltegger & Wagner, 2011; Shepherd & Patzelt, 2011) that integrate both environmental and social dimensions. As Muñoz and Dimov (2015, p. 641) articulate, this integrated perspective reflects "underlying attitudes and convictions towards environmental protection and social responsibility".

Developing on the latter holistic approach, the construct of SO has become a critical, foundational, and deeply embedded pillar in the development of the expanded entrepreneurial strategic posture of HEO (Parente et al., 2018; Vesci et al., 2024). Within HumEnt, SO is not positioned as an ancillary or supplementary element but rather as a defining component of the firm's identity and strategic intent – what it means to operate as a "humane" organization. Consequently, this perspective reframes the role of these entrepreneurs: they are viewed not only as conventional opportunity-seekers but also as stewards of ecological and social systems. Their responsibility extends to generating value that fundamentally transcends purely financial returns, incorporating broader societal and environmental benefits.

2.2.3 HRO: expanding the entrepreneurial strategic posture incorporating sympathetic relationships with workers

The HRO defines the strategic magnitude of entrepreneurial behaviour focused on cultivating supportive and ethical relationships with both employees and executives (Parente et al., 2021; Vesci et al., 2024, 2025). HRO is underpinned by three essential objectives: (a) the strategic behaviour to avoiding all forms of discrimination, (b) the strategic optimization of the workforce's potential and idea's generation (e.g., granting high levels of autonomy in work methods and encouraging free inquiry for organizational betterment), and (c) the strategic establishment of appropriate and equitable employment conditions (Kim et al., 2018). This conceptualization positions HRO as the most novel and distinguishing dimension characterizing both HumEnt and the resultant HEO. The foundational basis for HRO was established by Kim et al. (2018), who synthesized principles from the human resource management theory (Guest et al., 2000; Pfeffer, 1998) and the humanistic management approach (Melé, 2003; Spitzeck, 2011) to delineate four interconnected components:

1 empathy, which represents the strategic capacity of the enterprise to engage in a perspective to understand the values, motivations, and affective states of its employees (Choi, 2006; Kim et al., 2018);
2 equity, which is "the extent to which a company treats individuals in a fair and equal manner" (Kim et al., 2018, p. 19);
3 enablement, which symbolizes the degree to which an organization furnishes a conducive environment for individual skill and knowledge development (Jun et al., 2018; Kim et al., 2018);
4 empowerment, which aims to amplify employee motivation, foster deeper participation in decision-making, and leverage employee engagement for comprehensive enterprise development (Kim et al., 2018).

2.3 The characteristics of the Humane Entrepreneur behaviour

Being the Humane Entrepreneur a specific expression of HumEnt and acquired that HumEnt articulates a behavioural model of entrepreneurship rooted in EO (Covin & Slevin, 1989), the Humane Entrepreneur is not characterized by attributes or traits but is better signified through his strategic behaviour. Thus, the Humane Entrepreneur is that entrepreneur who demonstrates an Individual Humane Entrepreneurial Orientation (IHEO). In line with what we have recalled above about HEO (Parente et al., 2021; Vesci et al., 2023, 2024), IHEO is conceived as a strategic posture that measures at individual-level entrepreneurial orientation, SO, and HRO. Given that an organization, particularly one that is small, can be conceptually viewed as an extension or manifestation of the founder's individual behaviours (Hambrick & Mason, 1984), the dimensions of HEO can plausibly be measured at the individual level. For instance, individuals can be certainly observed as displaying degrees of innovativeness propensity or as high or low in risk aversion. Similarly, individuals demonstrate a certain level of taking care of environmental and social issues or individual can be more empathetic or not. Consequently, the application of HEO dimensions to the individual level not only is conceptually plausible but also holds significant theoretical and practical value. Specifically, assessing these individual behavioural patterns enlarges HEO magnitude introducing the individual level of measurement, supports the identification of values behind HEO, and helps in the design of more effective instructional methods tailored to possibly exhibited humane entrepreneurial tendencies of students.

In sum, the Humane Entrepreneur adopts an entrepreneurial strategic posture manifested through EO (Covin & Slevin, 1989), SO (Parente et al., 2021; Vesci et al., 2024) and HRO (Kim et al., 2018). It means that to have an entrepreneurial strategic posture, the mandatory condition derived from HumEnt theory is to demonstrate individually high levels of EO. Without high level of EO, no "entrepreneurial" posture could be recognized according to HumEnt. In parallel, the Humane Entrepreneur demonstrates at individual level also high levels of SO and HRO. This position means also that at individual level it is possible to find different combinations of high EO level and SO or HRO levels. In particular, it is possible to distinguish three different sub-profiles of Humane Entrepreneurs, demonstrating different characteristics:

1 The Humane Entrepreneurs transitioning to HRO;
2 The Humane Entrepreneurs transitioning to SO;
3 Ambiguous Humane Entrepreneurs.

The Humane Entrepreneurs transitioning to HRO exhibit strong levels of EO and SO but display lower levels of HRO. Conversely, those transitioning to SO demonstrate high levels of EO and HRO while showing low levels of SO. It means the Humane Entrepreneurs transitioning to HRO are entrepreneurs for sure having a clear behaviour oriented toward risk and innovation but do not have absorbed completely HumEnt posture because they only demonstrate behaviour finalized to taking care for environment and community. In this sub-profile of Humane Entrepreneur, taking care for humane-resource is substantially lacking. Similarly, Humane Entrepreneurs transitioning to SO are entrepreneurs for sure because they have a clear behaviour oriented toward risk and innovation given the high level of EO but do not have fully grasped HumEnt posture, demonstrating only a clear care for humane-resource but not for environment and society at large. In this sub-profile of Humane Entrepreneur, the care for sustainability is substantially absent. Finally, Ambiguous Humane Entrepreneurs show high levels of EO and ambiguous (not low) levels for both SO and HRO. In this case, given the clear entrepreneurial posture associated with high level of EO, the care for environmental concerns, for local communities, and for humane-resource is not fully nor totally displayed. This type of HE moves around taking care for environment, society, and humane-resource without conviction. Referring to these kinds of behaviour, they stay just in the middle. Their behaviour is not in total disregard of both environmental concern and care for employees, nor their behaviour is however clearly conceived for sustainability and humane-resource taking care.

2.4 The decision-making of the Humane Entrepreneur: the emerging role of personal values and beliefs

Recently, some scholars, integrating the Recognition-Primed Decision (RPD) theory (Klein, 1993, 2008, 2015), which represents the physical decision process, with Entrepreneurial Motivation – EM (Haynie et al., 2010; Randolph-Seng et al., 2015), which represents the mental decision process, introduced a broader and more comprehensive perspective of entrepreneurial decision-making (De Winnaar & Scholtz, 2020). RPD (Klein, 2008, 2015) emphasizes how decision-makers – especially those facing high levels of unpredictability, as entrepreneurs do – rely on experience to quickly recognize patterns and situational cues. Instead of generating and comparing multiple options, the experienced decision-maker (1) recognizes the situation as familiar or partially familiar; (2) identifies a plausible course of action based on this recognition; and (3) mentally simulates the action to ensure its workability. EM (Haynie et al., 2010; Randolph-Seng et al., 2015) encompasses the internal drive that influences direction, power, and perseverance of an entrepreneur's behaviour. When entrepreneurs encounter novel situations or those outside their routine, the selection of metacognitive strategies is profoundly influenced by the environmental context and the entrepreneur's internal drive (which governs the direction, intensity, and persistence of behaviour) (Haynie et al., 2010; Klein, 2015).

Applying these contentions, the Humane Entrepreneurs' decision-making process is clearly induced by familiarity with the situation and above all with entrepreneur's internal values. In particular, core values of the Humane Entrepreneurs fundamentally serve as the bedrock for their actions. This point is strictly in line with HumEnt propositions (Parente et al., 2018). Consequently, variations in individual-level values, beliefs, and orientations are supposed to influence entrepreneurial decision-making. Along this vein, Agle et al. (1999)

propose that strategic decisions incorporate sustainability issues based on the core values of the decision-maker within the organization. Empirical evidence supports this, as Jahanshahi et al. (2017, p. 2) observed that entrepreneurs characterized by a "strong belief in a just world and high future-orientation" are more likely to engage in sustainability-oriented entrepreneurial actions. Parente et al. (2018), proposing their HumEnt model, identified entrepreneurs' personal values, such as spirituality and religiosity or more in general personal credos regarding sustainability issues and how to take care of human resources, as external factors that enable the humane entrepreneurial strategic posture. In sum, the Humane Entrepreneurs' decision-making appears to be fundamentally rooted in the personal values and cultural background of the entrepreneurs themselves. Specifically, this combination of values and culture represented by entrepreneur's sensibility towards sustainability and humane-resources concerns seems to foster a visionary framework or scenario. This overarching vision is subsequently adopted by the Humane Entrepreneur, who then leverage it to effectively implement and exploit the core business idea initially conceived. Thus, familiarity with the situation plays a clear role in boosting the decision-making towards adoption.

2.5 Discussion and conclusion

The Humane Entrepreneur emerges as specific profile of entrepreneurship with a specific behaviour and a specific decision-making process.

In particular, the "Humane" feature, that is rooted in the HumEnt theory, identifies a behaviour characterized by the strategical consideration of sustainability concerns and by the adoption of strategic stance to better employee engagement and enablement with humanistic modes (Parente et al., 2018, 2021; Vesci et al., 2023, 2025). However, the basic characteristic of the Humane Entrepreneur is to behave not in a conservative manner but entrepreneurially or, more clearly, respecting the position of Covin and Slevin (1989), assuming a certain level of (financial) risk, innovating, and being proactive. Along this vein, the Humane Entrepreneur is not identified by specific attributes and what matters is only his concrete behaviour. It is consequentially clear that not all entrepreneurs are Humane Entrepreneurs and that there is not a predefined journey towards HumEnt. In the realm of business, it will be possible to find classic entrepreneurs that are only risky and innovation oriented or Humane Entrepreneurs that have just started their journey (e.g., Humane Entrepreneurs in transition) given the actions put in place to taking care of sustainability concerns or alternatively given the actions put in place for engaging and enabling employees with humane modes (Vesci et al., 2024). At the same time, the realm of business can offer Humane Entrepreneurs that are ambiguous having embraced the Humane posture without conviction.

Regarding decision-making, the "Humane" feature, adopting RPD and EM as lens for understanding, creates a kind of specificity because of the entrepreneur's personal credos and values. In fact, while the process carried out by the Humane Entrepreneur could overlap with other types of entrepreneurs, specific values of the Humane Entrepreneur enable a different way to approach entrepreneurship. In fact, when the Humane Entrepreneur makes choices, he activates, especially in unfamiliar situation, his own (cultural or religious) values, promoting a different approach to entrepreneurship in respect to traditional entrepreneur. In this way, he enables a scenario that takes into consideration environmental and local communities' concerns as well as employees' empowerment and empathetic relationship with them.

Although, as said HumEnt approach is not generalizable, the Humane Entrepreneur profile opens new avenues for research with a plethora of research questions to answer. What are the drivers and personal values that better influence the Humane Entrepreneur? Which are the conditions that enable better performance for these drivers? What are the differences with the social entrepreneur? In which way is it possible to measure the IHEO? Is the Humane Entrepreneur a question of Small Businesses or Large Corporations? Which are the dimensions that push forward the Humane Entrepreneur in transition?

In sum, the Humane Entrepreneur is a new profile of entrepreneur that was born at the dawn of the twenty-first century and it is clear that its theoretical basis is still in their infancy. This profile is not for all entrepreneurship nor for all scenarios. But "Humane" and "Humanity" are taking traction in several fields, also in entrepreneurship. So, the journey towards HumEnt is started: it is up to us as academics to push it forward discussing it!

References

Agle, B. R., Mitchell, R. K., Sonnenfeld, J. A. (1999). Who matters to CEOs? An investigation of stakeholder attributes and salience, corporate performance, and CEO values. *The Academy of Management Journal*, 42(5), 507–525.

Baumol, W. J. (1968). Entrepreneurship in economic theory. *American Economic Review*, 58(2), 64–71.

Baumol, W. J. (1990). Entrepreneurship: productive, unproductive, and destructive. *Journal of Political Economy*, 98, 893–921.

Baumol, W. J. (1994). *Entrepreneurship, Management and the Structure of Payoffs*. MIT Press, Cambridge.

Belz, F. M., Binder, J. K. (2017). Sustainable entrepreneurship: a convergent process model. *Business Strategy and the Environment*, 26(1), 1–17.

Botti, A., Parente, R. (Eds.). (2024). *Humane Entrepreneurship and Innovation* (Emerald Studies in Sustainable Innovation Management). Emerald Publishing Limited, Leeds.

Business Roundtable (2019). *Statement on the Purpose of a Corporation*. Available at: https://opportunity.businessroundtable.org/wp-content/uploads/2019/12/BRT-Statement-on-the-Purpose-of-a-Corporation-with-Signatures.pdf.

Chen, C. C., Greene, P. G., Crick, A. (1998). Does entrepreneurial self-efficacy distinguish entrepreneurs from managers? *Journal of Business Venturing*, 13(4), 295–316.

Choi, J. (2006). A motivational theory of charismatic leadership: envisioning, empathy, and empowerment. *Journal of Leadership and Organizational Studies*, 13(1), 24–43.
Covin, J. G., Lumpkin, G. T. (2011). Entrepreneurial orientation theory and research: reflections on a needed construct. *Entrepreneurship Theory and Practice*, 35(5), 855–872.
Covin, J. G., Slevin, D. P. (1989). Strategic management of small firms in hostile and benign environments. *Strategic Management Journal*, 10(1), 75–87.
Covin, J. G., Slevin, D. P. (1990). New venture strategic posture, structure, and performance: an industry life cycle analysis. *Journal of Business Venturing*, 5(2), 123–135.
Covin, J. G., Slevin, D. P. (1991). A conceptual model of entrepreneurship as firm behavior. *Entrepreneurship Theory and Practice*, 16(1), 7–25.
De Clercq, D., Voronov, M. (2011). Sustainability in entrepreneurship: a tale of two logics. *International Small Business Journal*, 29, 322–344.
De Winnaar, K., Scholtz, F. (2020). Entrepreneurial decision-making: new conceptual perspectives. *Management Decision*, 58(7), 1283–1300.
Guest, D. E., Michie, J., Sheehan, M., Conway, N., Metochi, M. (2000). *Effective People Management: Initial Findings of the Future of Work Survey*. Chartered Institute of Personnel and Development (CIPD), London.
Hambrick, D. C., Mason, P. A. (1984). Upper echelons: the organization as a reflection of its top managers. *The Academy of Management Review*, 9(2), 193–206.
Haynie, J. M., Shepherd, D., Mosakowski, E., Earley, P. C. (2010). A situated metacognitive model of the entrepreneurial mindset. *Journal of Business Venturing*, 25(2), 217–229.
Jahanshahi, A. A., Brem, A., Bhattacharjee, A. (2017). Who takes more sustainability-oriented entrepreneurial actions? The role of entrepreneurs' values, beliefs and orientations. *Sustainability*, 9, 1636, 1–19.
Jun, J., Kim, K. C., Song, C. S., Enriquez, J. L. (2018). Humane orientation at entrepreneurship: concept, measurement, and effect – how does empathy and empowerment affect EO and business performance? *ICSB World Conference Proceedings*. Washington, DC.
Kim, K. C., El Tarabishy, A., Bae, Z. T. (2018). Humane entrepreneurship: how focusing on people can drive a new era of wealth and quality job creation in a sustainable world. *Journal of Small Business Management*, 56(S1), 10–29.
Kim, K. C., Hornsby, J. S., Enriquez, J. L., Bae, Z. T., El Tarabishy, A. (2021). Humane Entrepreneurial Framework: a model for effective corporate entrepreneurship. *Journal of Small Business Management*, 59(3), 397–416.
Kirzner, I. M. (1973). *Competition and Entrepreneurship*. University of Chicago Press, Chicago, IL.
Kirzner, I. M. (1979). *Perception, Opportunity, and Profit*. University of Chicago Press, Chicago, IL.
Klein, G. (1993). *A Recognition-Primed Decision (RPD) Model of Rapid Decision Making*. Ablex Publishing Corporation, New York.
Klein, G. (2008). Naturalistic decision making. *Human Factors: The Journal of the Human Factors and Ergonomics Society*, 50(3), 456–460.
Klein, G. (2015). A naturalistic decision-making perspective on studying intuitive decision making. *Journal of Applied Research in Memory and Cognition*, 4(3), 164–168.
Linnanen, L. (2002). An insider's experience with environmental entrepreneurship. *Greener Management International*, 38, 71–80.

Lumpkin, G. T., Moss, T. W., Gras, D. M., Kato, S., Amezcua, A. S. (2013). Entrepreneurial processes in social contexts: hoy are they different, if at all? *Small Business Economics*, 40, 761–783.

Melé, D. (2003). The challenge of humanistic management. *Journal of Business Ethics*, 44, 77–88.

Muñoz, P., Dimov, D. (2015). The call of the whole in understanding the development of sustainable ventures. *Journal of Business Venturing*, 30(4), 632–654.

O'Neill, K., Gibbs, D. (2016). Rethinking green entrepreneurship. Fluid narratives of the green economy. *Environment and Planning A: Economy and Space*, 48(9), 1727–1749.

Parente, R., El Tarabishy, A., Botti, A., Vesci, M., Feola, R. (2021). Humane entrepreneurship: some steps in the development of a measurement scale. *Journal of Small Business Management*, 59(3), 509–533.

Parente, R., El Tarabishy, A., Vesci, M. Botti, A. (2018). The epistemology of humane entrepreneurship: theory and proposal for future research agenda. *Journal of Small Business Management*, 56(S1), 30–52.

Parente, R., Kim, K. C. (2021). Editorial: contemporary perspectives on social and humane entrepreneurship. *Journal of Small Business Management*, 59(3), 371–372.

Pfeffer, J. (1998). *The Human Equation: Building Profits by Putting People First*. Harvard Business School, Boston, MA.

Randolph-Seng, B., Mitchell, R. K., Vahidnia, H., Mitchell, J. R., Chen, S., Statzer, J. (2015). The microfoundations of entrepreneurial cognition research: toward an integrative approach. *Foundations and Trends® in Entrepreneurship*, 11(4), 207–335.

Schaltegger, S., Wagner, M. (2011). Sustainable entrepreneurship and sustainability innovation: categories and interactions. *Business Strategy and the Environment*, 20(4), 222–237.

Schumpeter, J. A. (1934). *The Theory of Economic Development*. Harvard University Press, Cambridge.

Shane, S., Venkataraman, S. (2000). The promise of entrepreneurship as a field of research. *Academy of Management Review*, 25(1), 217–226.

Shepherd, D. A., Patzelt, H. (2011). The new field of sustainable entrepreneurship: studying entrepreneurial action linking "what is to be sustained" with what is to be developed. *Entrepreneurship Theory and Practice*, 35(1), 137–163.

Spitzeck, H. (2011). An integrated model of humanistic management. *Journal of Business Ethics*, 99, 51–62.

United Nations. (2015). *Resolution Adopted by the General Assembly on 25 September 2015*. Available at: https://www.un.org/en/development/desa/population/migration/generalassembly/docs/globalcompact/A_RES_70_1_E.pdf (accessed November 13, 2025).

Vesci, M., Botti, A., Feola, R., Conti, E., El Tarabishy, A. (2023), Bridging theory and practice in the humane entrepreneurship domain: insights from small and medium Italian enterprises. *Journal of Small Business and Enterprise Development*, 30(3), 567–586.

Vesci, M., Botti, A., Parente, R. (2024). The humane entrepreneurship framework. In A. Botti, R. Parente (Eds.), *Humane Entrepreneurship and Innovation* (Emerald Studies in Sustainable Innovation Management), Emerald Publishing Limited, Leeds (pp. 89–103).

Vesci, M., Feola, R., Parente, R., Botti, A. (2025). Does humane entrepreneurship have value? Exploring the link between employees' beliefs and firm financial performance: a perceptual approach. *International Entrepreneurship and Management Journal*. DOI: 10.1007/s11365-025-01151-z.

Zahra, S. A., Gedajlovic, E., Neubaum, D. O., Shulman, J. M. (2009). A typology of social entrepreneurs: motives, search processes and ethical challenges. *Journal of Business Venturing*, 24(5), 519–532.

3 The sapiens entrepreneur

Diego Matricano

3.1 How was the concept conceived?

In an attempt to approach entrepreneurship studies from an interdisciplinary perspective, capable of viewing this complex phenomenon through new lenses and improving the results achieved (Matricano, 2023), various theories, principles, approaches, frameworks, concepts, or constructs are borrowed from other disciplines and fields of knowledge. Despite the risk of an invasion of other disciplines into entrepreneurship and of an unbalanced relationship between them (Corley & Gioia, 2011; Okhuysen & Bonardi, 2011), a review of some foundations of entrepreneurship has been conducted (Matricano, 2015, 2024). Obviously, many topics are fundamental to entrepreneurship and the ones considered here do not claim to be unanimously accepted. However, they are certainly rooted in the field and have assumed a significant role in this area of research.

Individual abilities to respond to, anticipate, or predict the future (Knight, 1921) are the first fundamental principle considered here. This ability can be explored and interpreted by drawing on the original theory of dynamic capabilities (Teece et al., 1997) and transposing it to entrepreneurship (Boccardelli & Magnusson, 2006; Matricano, 2025a; Teece, 2023; Zahra et al., 2006). As is well known, dynamic capabilities do not concern specific variables (knowledge, experience, or behaviour) but rather the outcomes of interactions and exchanges. Dynamic Capabilities in Entrepreneurship – DyCE (Matricano, 2025a, 2025b) can describe how individuals and their networks integrate, build, and reconfigure internal and external capabilities to address rapidly changing environments (Teece et al., 1997). This concept can capture how a set of variables evolves – not each of them but all of them.

Another fundamental that is considered here deals with entrepreneurial opportunities and their recognition, discovery, and creation (Alvarez & Barney, 2007; Ireland et al., 2001; Sarasvathy et al., 2005; Shane, 2003). Since the maturity level of entrepreneurial opportunities cannot be measured absolutely and objectively, the concept of *likeability bias* (Matricano, 2024), rooted in psychology and gender studies (Moreno-Gata et al., 2024; Pinto

DOI: 10.4324/9781003681182-3

et al., 2015), could be used. This is a subjective assessment (not an accurate measurement) that depends on each stakeholder. Entrepreneurs constantly work on their opportunities to simultaneously adapt them to the expectations of different stakeholders (Matricano, 2024).

Still another fundamental concerns the external context. This is characterized by true uncertainty (Knight, 1921), is unknown and unknowable (Bryan et al., 2022; Dimov, 2018; Loch et al., 2008), and leaves entrepreneurs with no room for speculation. It is volatile, uncertain, complex, and ambiguous – VUCA (Scheibel et al., 2025; Wang et al., 2022). Therefore, entrepreneurs must consider various aspects of the context (e.g., environmental, social, and economic) and assess how these aspects may change over time. Consequently, they are expected to act in a continuous effort to balance them. This is called the quest for balance.

Considering the DyCE, the likeability bias, and the quest for balance, entrepreneurs are expected to adopt a new posture that allows them to manage relevant variables and their evolution. This posture or attitude, borrowed from philosophy and classical studies (Small, 2013; Williams, 1990), is based on Seneca's concept of *sapientia* and assumes that entrepreneurs must practise wisdom combined with careful discernment in their judgements and actions. Before shifting the concepts of *sapientia* and *sapiens* from philosophy and classical studies to entrepreneurship, it is essential to retrace their origins.

3.2 The origin of sapientia and *sapiens*

The story begins not with wisdom in the grand philosophical sense but with a more primal, sensory experience. The Latin verb *sapere* initially meant to taste, to have flavour. Shily, there was a sematic shift to cognition, and so the verb *sapere* evolved to mean 'to be wise, to discern, to understand'. The shift is intuitive: just as one discerns flavours with the palate, one discerns truths with the mind. To have 'good taste' in matters of truth and judgement is to be wise. As time passed by, two words derived from the verb *sapere*: *sapientia*, standing for wisdom, a quality assigned to individuals, and *sapiens*, standing for wise, discerning, rational individuals who embody these qualities.

After this initial stage, the Latin verb *sapere* has been evolving in different fields from knowledge (from philosophy to science and biology) and with different meanings in the same field. In this case, we are going to stay in the field of philosophy and, in particular, we are going to compare the Greek and Latin philosophy. Although using different words, ancient Greek philosophy established the core ideas that would then be translated into the Latin sapientia. In particular, as remarked by Rorty (1978) and Long (2002), Aristotle (in his *Nicomachean Ethics*, written around 322 B.C.) made a crucial distinction between *sophia* (theoretical wisdom, referring to knowledge of eternal and fundamental truths, e.g., metaphysics, mathematics) and *phronesis* (practical wisdom, referring to the ability to deliberate well about what is good and beneficial for life). Centuries later, the Latin term *sapientia* came to encompass both, but with a strong emphasis on the theoretical, eternal realm. In particular, as remarked by Hansen (2018), Seneca (in his *De Constantia Sapientis*, written around 55 A.C.) meant *sapientia* as the highest good, the state of living in accordance with nature and reason. The *sapiens* was the ideal sage, who had achieved perfect rationality and was free from the passions that disturb ordinary people.

Without getting to the view authored by St. Thomas Aquinas and proposed in his *Summa Theologiae*, written between 1266 and 1273, where the scholar synthesizes Aristotelian thought with Christian theology and considers *sapientia* as the highest of the intellectual virtues, representing judgement through ultimate causes and culminating in the knowledge of God (Morrissey, 2012), it is interesting to deepen the view of *sapientia* as a pinnacle of human intellectual and moral achievement to attain.

According to Seneca, in fact, the concept of *sapiens* presents a pragmatic and attainable model. The *sapiens*, who is not immune to the passions, learns to master them through reason. The *sapiens* practises political and personal coherence and is committed to continuous improvement, living a daily ethical path oriented toward wisdom. The greatness assigned to this individual does not lie in his contempt for joys and sorrows but in his ability to manage them. In fact, what is most striking in Seneca's description is the journey to wisdom. The *sapiens* embarks on a path of constant growth that involves daily self-examination to identify one's flaws and correct them through daily commitment, diligence in education, and self-control. In fact, in Seneca's view, the *sapiens* is not an unattainable ideal but a realistic model of behaviour to apply in everyday life and social contexts. For Seneca, true greatness consists in knowing how to master human feelings (joy and sorrow, happiness, and fear) with reason.

Before concluding, it must be admitted that wisdom is not the ultimate goal Seneca assigns to individuals. This is the inner freedom that belongs to the wise. Of course, this note takes the concepts of *sapiens* and *sapientia* far from the field of entrepreneurship, and this generates the risk of being off topic. For this reason, attention here is focused on commitment, diligence in education, and self-control that lead to master human feelings with reason.

3.3 The characteristics of the *sapiens* entrepreneurs

In line with the definitions recalled above, the seminal definition (Matricano, 2024, p. 3119) argues that the "sapiens entrepreneurs should assume a posture based on wisdom combined with careful discernment in judging and in operating". This statement must be read as a whole since it clarifies the leverage and the goal attributed to these entrepreneurs but, at the same time, each word in it deserves huge attention. In particular, attention must be paid to the posture to adopt, the concepts of wisdom and discernment, and the activities of judgement and action.

Let us start with posture. Generally, this can be defined as the position of the body in space that maintains balance during both dynamic movements and static situations. According to the basic notions of physiotherapy, it represents the body's automatic and unconscious reaction to the force of gravity. It is maintained through coordinated skeletal muscle contractions and continuous neuromuscular adjustments. Essentially, posture is any position that achieves balance with maximum stability, minimal energy consumption, and minimal stress on anatomical structures.

According to the contexts in previous lines, three key concepts are at the basis of posture: (1) spatiality, i.e., body position in three-dimensional space and relationships between skeletal segments; (2) anti-gravity response, i.e., posture as a reaction to the fundamental external force of gravity; (3) balance, i.e., the relationship between the subject and environment. Specifically, balance can be static (maintaining a stationary position with the spinal column stretched upwards along the centre of gravity) or dynamic (maintaining stability during daily activities). Both dynamic and static balance require a person to maintain their centre of gravity through anatomical structures while using antagonistic isometric muscle contractions that create postural tone. This postural tone can be functional (if it is characterized by the absence of pain and harmonious skeletal segment relationships) or non-functional (if it is marked by pain and muscle dystonia).

The transposition of this concept from the field of physiotherapy to the field of entrepreneurship invites to think about how entrepreneurs relate to the context they are in (Gaddefors & Anderson, 2017; Welter, 2011). Spatiality, anti-gravity response, and balance are the three key concepts that determine the posture and – in reference to entrepreneurship – can express how individuals relate to and face market issues. By positioning themselves according to a three-dimensional perspective (spatiality), by reacting to external forces (anti-gravity response), and by relating to the context in a proper way (balance), entrepreneurs are pushed to define their plans and actions[1] in order to remain standing.

As a matter of fact, it is not just important to stand, but it is also important how. Entrepreneurs must define how to approach the context since this allows them to keep a functional posture in the long term. As already said, posture can be functional (if it is characterized by the absence of pain and harmonious skeletal segment relationships) or non-functional (if it is marked by pain and muscle dystonia) in the field of physiotherapy. The difference is in the absence or presence of pain when standing. What does this mean in reference to entrepreneurship? It means that entrepreneurs must adopt a positive feeling as the basis of their standing, judging, and acting. What does this mean in practical terms? Entrepreneurship literature teaches us that the context is characterized by true uncertainty (Knight, 1921). It is unknown and unknowable (Dimov, 2018; Parker, 2006; Townsend et al., 2018), VUCA (Santoso et al., 2020; Scheibel et al., 2025), and does not allow entrepreneurs any conjecture.

Accordingly, entrepreneurs must consider different aspects of the context (for example, environmental, social, and economic) and evaluate how these aspects may change over time before making any decision. According to the concepts of *sapiens* and *sapientia*, i.e., that entrepreneurs can master their feelings with reason, it is reasonable to expect that entrepreneurs can analyse the context in a proper way and, consequently, judge and act in a continuous effort to balance the different aspects of the context (quest for balance), which means minimizing negative conditions (pains) and maximizing positive circumstances (gains). This view clarifies that wisdom and discernment are the criteria that should lead the *sapiens* entrepreneurs' judgements and actions (Matricano, 2024).

Posture, wisdom, and discernment shape the processes put into practice by the *sapiens* entrepreneurs, as explained in the next section.

3.4 The process carried out by the *sapiens* entrepreneurs

Before analysing how the *sapiens* entrepreneurs manage their processes, by judging and acting, it is mandatory to rebuild a hypothetical structure of entrepreneurship processes.

Over the years, scholars have proposed many contributions (Davidsson & Gruenhagen, 2021; Moroz & Hindle, 2012; Steyaert 2007). Moroz and Hindle (2012) went through and classified them according to five categories: stage models, static frameworks, process dynamics, quantification sequences, and others. In reference to the *sapiens* entrepreneurs, who act with wisdom and discernment to assume and maintain a define posture, the first category (dealing with stage models and dividing entrepreneurship processes into a priori stages or major tasks (Moroz & Hindle, 2012)), sounds interesting. In this wake, other contributions have been read to verify if they contain stages or major tasks. The results are presented in Table 3.1.

All the papers cited above cannot be compared as each of them deals with a specific aspect of the entrepreneurship process. However, two can be of major interest for this study as they focus on macro-phases, which are more or less manifest or more often recalled in all the papers. These contributions are authored by Baron (2007) and Baron and Henry (2011). According to the scholars, all entrepreneurship processes are made up of three major phases (Baron, 2007). These are the prelaunch, launch, and postlaunch phases. The duration of these major phases can vary as they comprehend various activities and related sub-phases and several individual-, group-, and societal-level variables that entrepreneurs must orchestrate. It is up to entrepreneurs to make decisions and move from one phase to another.

In summary, regarding the entrepreneurial process (understood as its structure and sequence of phases), the *sapiens* entrepreneurs do not look at it differently from other entrepreneurs. However, the approach to decision-making

Table 3.1 A review of contributions focused on entrepreneurship processes

Contributions	*The model contribution focuses on…*
Hornsby et al. (1993)	Intrapreneurship and entrepreneurship
Bhave (1994)	Entrepreneurial opportunities
Bygrave (2004)	Stages and variables to test
Baker and Nelson (2005)	Bricolage
Corbett (2005)	Learning
Jones and Coviello (2005)	Internationalization
Baron (2007)	Macro-phases and groups of variables
Cunneen et al. (2007)	Growth
Fayolle (2007)	Learning and education
Slotte-Kock and Coviello (2010)	Network
Additional papers, not included in Moroz and Hindle's contribution (2011):	
Baker et al. (2005)	International comparison
Ruef (2005)	Stages and variables to test
Heinonen and Poikkijoki (2006)	Education
Haber and Reichel (2007)	Tourism
Baron and Henry (2012)	Key aspects
Gielnik et al. (2015)	Entrepreneurial passion
Leyden and Link (2015)	Opportunity discovery/creation and network
Held et al. (2018)	Team formation
Lévesque and Stephan (2020)	Time
Gieure et al. (2020)	Intentions and behaviour
Guerrero et al. (2021)	Ecosystem
Wood et al. (2021)	Time
Davidsson and Gruenhagen (2021)	'the process within the process'
Wang et al. (2022)	The role of artificial intelligence during processes
Bennett and Chatterji (2023)	The pre-entry period
Lyu et al. (2024)	Entrepreneurial opportunities
Baron (2024)	Interdisciplinarity
Williams et al. (2024)	Resources
Matricano (2025b)	Dynamic capabilities

Source: Author's personal elaboration.

is different. For this reason, it is interesting to shift attention to decisional mechanisms and identify the peculiarities of the *sapiens* entrepreneurs.

3.5 Making *sapiens* decisions

After revealing the characteristics of the *sapiens* entrepreneurs and the structure/sequence of the phases that define entrepreneurship processes, it is interesting to speculate on how they go through them. More specifically, it is attractive to conjecture how they select the best means-ends relationships.

Entrepreneurs can use two approaches: a simultaneous and a sequential one (Sleptsov & Anand, 2008). Both have strengths and weaknesses.

By adopting a simultaneous approach, entrepreneurs try to evaluate many options at the same time. In this case, they are supposed to collect information and develop knowledge about all of them to compare them and, eventually, seize the best. The positive aspect of this approach is that options are selected through an 'absolute comparison' (Sleptsov & Anand, 2008, p. 361) which means that all the means-ends relationships are reflected upon at the same time. The negative aspect consists of reducing the amount and the quality of information and knowledge for each option, and this increases uncertainty.

By adopting a sequential approach, entrepreneurs decide whether to exploit one option by considering just that one. If they do not decide to exploit that option, then they start looking for another. The negative aspect of this procedure consists in realizing a 'relative comparison' (Sleptsov & Anand, 2008, p. 361). It means that an option is evaluated by itself, without comparing it to another. In an extreme hypothesis, it might happen that an individual can realize that an option is better than another only after rejecting the first one; this recalls the concept of path-dependence (David, 2000). This hypothesis is rare since entrepreneurs, before rejecting an option, are supposed to get detailed information and a deeper knowledge. This is the positive aspect of this approach.

Actually, this logical distinction does not seem useful since entrepreneurs cannot define the number of options to evaluate *a priori*. For this reason, it is important to recall the contribution provided by Eckhardt and Ciuchta (2008) who define decision-making as a not ordered and non-irreversible sequence. These features make the process very complex as entrepreneurs can go back and redefine their choices several times. It is like admitting that the entrepreneurship process can restart and, of course, the approach can always change from simultaneous to sequential and vice versa.

This note paves the way to the proposal of a multistage model (Eckhardt et al., 2006), consisting of selecting an option in subsequent phases, which determine the final choice. This means that the output of a previous phase influences the output of the next, so the capabilities required to make each decision may change. Does the multistage model simplify the decision-making? For sure, this model offers a more realistic description of entrepreneurship processes but – at the same time – reveals its complexity.

In the multistage model, in fact, the concepts of path-dependence (on the one hand) and of uncertainty and risk (on the other) become critical.

3.5.1 Path-dependence

The concept of path-dependence (David, 2000) assumes that every choice is the result of the experiences lived in the past. As formerly stated by David himself (1985), previous events can cause relevant consequences that behaviour can partially modify. Previous events, in fact, can generate the *status* of locked-in or locked-out.

The lock-in theory (David, 2000; Barnes et al., 2004) refers to the cases when an agent enters a decisional area from which it is difficult to get out unless external forces or shocks occur. Referring the theory to the decisional process, the path that an individual has already walked will lead to certain situations and future choices. These are the result of what has already happened. To some extent, it is like saying situations are predetermined by what has been done and are not so easily modifiable without external forces. Then, at the moment of choosing, individuals are supposed to be locked in a given set of alternatives between which they can choose, but they cannot evaluate other alternatives beyond those.

Instead, the lock-out theory analyses what happens when agents get out of a decisional area (Cohen & Levinthal, 1990; Crespo et al., 2014). This theory is based on the idea that, because of the previous path, some signals were not considered as they should or, in extreme cases, they were wrongly considered as meaningless. In this case, situations that could be positive for individuals are not included in the decisional area, and so they will never be caught or evaluated.

In both cases, the main limit of path-dependence consists of impeding an effective evaluation of options because it locks individuals into a defined *status* from which it is difficult to escape.

3.5.2 Uncertainty

Before dealing with uncertainty, it is mandatory to clarify its relationship with risk. Some scholars (Hmielesky & Baron, 2008; Knight, 1921) view uncertainty and risk as two different concepts, while other scholars (Gifford, 2005; Khilstrom & Laffont, 1979) consider uncertainty as implying risk. Gifford (2005, p. 37), for example, analyses the role of 'uncertainty and the accompanying risk'. In this case, uncertainty is the independent variable generating some implications, and risk is one of them.

For a start, uncertainty needs to be defined, and Knight's contribution (1921) proves very helpful. The scholar distinguishes three kinds of uncertainty. The first refers to 'a future whose distribution exists and is known'. All the events, which are expected to happen in the future, are already known, so the individual can easily reduce this kind of uncertainty through diversification. Economic agents, in fact, can evaluate different scenarios, foresee all the possible events, and choose accordingly. This kind of uncertainty is very easy to reduce. The second kind of uncertainty, instead, is generated by 'a future whose distribution exists but is not known in advance'. This kind of uncertainty is due to the fact that future events can be hypothesized after several trials, but they can never be formalized. Reducing uncertainty, in this case, is not easy. Individuals, in fact, are not supposed to foresee what is going to happen, so all the changes are seen as if they would happen for the first time. The third kind of uncertainty, the most difficult one to face, is the one that Knight explicitly calls 'true uncertainty'. According to Sarasvathy et al. (2005, p. 144), the concept of Knightian true uncertainty is so complex that the author himself 'did not explicate how the entrepreneur deals with this true uncertainty'. In fact, it is referred to a future which is 'unknown and unknowable'. The only reason why entrepreneurs decide to bear this uncertainty is that they expect to earn entrepreneurial profits.

'True uncertainty' is the most connected to entrepreneurial studies and so the most inquired. Following Knight's view, other scholars relate uncertainty to the impossibility of foreseeing future events (Duncan, 1972) or future outcomes (Downey & Slocum, 1975), while others identify uncertainty with the missing information about the cause-effect nexus (Lawrence & Lorsch, 1967). Several years later, Hmielesky and Baron (2008, p. 289) maintain that "a state of uncertainty occurs when the probabilities of decision outcomes cannot be estimated, because the necessary information is unknowable in the present". The relationship existing between uncertainty and entrepreneurship processes is very complex, and several views have been hypothesized over the years. Scholars (Shane & Venkataraman, 2000) agree on the fact that uncertainty may prevent individuals from making decisions. Fortunately, although entrepreneurs cannot follow 'relatively complete and unchanging' strategies to face uncertainty, they can define and adopt 'emergent and changing' strategies (Alvarez & Barney, 2007, p. 17). In fact, uncertainty causes impediments and opportunities as well (Companys & McMullen, 2007).

3.5.3 How can entrepreneurs cope with path-dependence and uncertainty? The emerging role of sapientia

Path-dependence and uncertainty do not allow entrepreneurs to evaluate new means-ends relationships and advance entrepreneurship processes straightforwardly. Processes could stop at any time because entrepreneurs cannot remove these limits. How can entrepreneurs overcome these limits? The only feasible way is to invest in human capital, i.e., to develop new capabilities and skills able to boost productivity and improve performance (Bowman & Swart, 2007; Ucbasaran et al., 2008).

Immediately, scholars have focused attention on who needs to invest in knowledge, how they do this, and which abilities can be improved.

It is not easy to investigate who could be more interested in investing in human capital. Based on the premise that all entrepreneurs should be interested in this, some of them could be more interested than others. Given for granted that those with more human capital are more able to reduce the implications of path-dependence and uncertainty, the problem is about the starting condition from which an individual should begin investing in knowledge.

An example can make this more readily understandable. All entrepreneurs can be divided into two different groups. Group A is made up of the ones with higher skills. Group B, instead, has lower skills. Both of them wish to have more human capital so they can reduce the negative effects of path-dependence and uncertainty. Group B will be the first to invest in human capital since they feel they need it. Gifford (2005, p. 48) writes "a person with fewer skills will be inclined to invest more in human capital. A person with higher skills will use those skills and invest less in human capital". Improvement of group B will push group A to do the same since the latter has lower skills now. So, even if Group A was not initially interested in investing, they are now. Ultimately, all aspiring entrepreneurs, whether highly skilled or less skilled, feel the need to improve their human capital.

As for the second topic, dealing with how entrepreneurs learn, a very interesting and useful example is provided by Gifford (2005) when he describes the story of the aspiring magician, who wants to launch a new career, similar to an entrepreneur. The aspiring magician, without previous experience, cannot convince others of his skills. To do that, he needs to follow a well-known magician in order to learn his skills by schooling, training, and direct experience (Cooper et al., 1989). Several years later, after the well-known magician could evaluate skills acquired by aspiring magician, both magicians can achieve great outcomes. In fact, the aspiring can perform in public and start his career, the well-known instead can attract more apprentices (pp. 42 ss). The story, which underlines how individual behaviour can influence or even determine the output of investments in human capital, recalls the way to do that and the limits that can impede that.

Besides the provided example, the learning process can take place in several ways: by using, by doing, by failing, by searching, by imitating, by interacting, and by cooperating (Corbett, 2005). In reference to the individual, the results deriving by all these ways of learning are unforeseeable because of 'limited attention' (Gifford, 2005, p. 38). Among the scarce resources an individual has to manage during the entrepreneurial process, in fact, attention is the most critical one. So, a right allocation of attention requires assigning it to all the activities so to get a deeper knowledge.

The third topic, about the abilities that can be improved, has been largely discussed among scholars (Winkler et al., 2023). In particular, learning helps to shape mental schemes and behavioural routines (Neergaard et al., 2021). Two abilities can be improved. The former is the ability to collect information. The latter is the ability to analyse the possessed information in the best way before acting. It is precisely in reference to this last point that *sapientia* comes into play.

As already said, according to Seneca's view, the *sapiens* entrepreneurs can master their passions through reason, express personal coherence, and are committed to continuous improvement, living a daily ethical path oriented toward wisdom. According to this perspective, entrepreneurship processes and related decisions are helpful for entrepreneurs to put into practice daily commitment, diligence in education, and self-control inspired by *sapientia*, i.e., by reason that governs the passions.

3.6 Discussion and conclusion

The emerging role of *sapientia* in entrepreneurship processes and decision-making and the consequent profile of the *sapiens* entrepreneurs partly overlap with previous theories and partly open new trajectories of research. In line with previous theories, also the *sapiens* entrepreneurs look at entrepreneurship as a 'process within the process' (Davidsson & Gruenhagen, 2021, p. 1094). Several steps, stages, and stops characterize the process. It is not possible to generalize whether decisions are simultaneous or sequential (Sleptsov & Anand, 2008). What matters is the final goal pursued. And here they are the new trajectories of research. By sharing the idea that reason can govern the passions, entrepreneurs admit they aspire to becoming ideal sages, with perfect rationality, personal coherence, and commitment to continuous improvement toward wisdom. Implicitly, the final goal they want to pursue is expected to go beyond personal and narrow goals. These, in fact, can be re-oriented because of a realistic model of behaviour applied in everyday life and social contexts and, in turn, take to social and widespread goals. The passions, causing ephemeral results, can be replaced by reason and ethics, which can push entrepreneurs to shape stronger ventures, lead them better, and make them last longer.

Of course, the process taking to sapientia cannot be generalized, and individuals need to walk along their paths and identify and correct their flaws to improve themselves. The same happens for entrepreneurs. It is not possible to generalize the entire journey towards *sapientia*, but the awareness of moving towards it is the right first step to take.

Note

1 About the evolution of the concept of posture in the field of entrepreneurship, it must be said that several scholars do not attribute it to individuals, but to firms and talk about strategic posture (Covin & Slevin, 1991; Kuratko et al., 2007). Plans and actions derive from the strategic posture and refer to the organizational implications of strategic posture. Over the years, strategic posture and its organizational implications have been referred to startups (Amankwah-Amoah et al., 2023), internationalisation processes (Thoumrungroje & Tansuhaj, 2005), or growth processes (McDonald, 2025).

References

Alvarez, S. A., Barney, J. B. (2007). Guest editors' introduction. The entrepreneurial theory of the firm. *Journal of Management Studies*, *44*(7), 1057–1063.

Amankwah-Amoah, J., Nyuur, R. B., Hinson, R., Kosiba, J. P., Al-Tabbaa, O., Cunningham, J. A. (2023). Entrepreneurial strategic posture and new technology ventures in an emerging economy. *International Journal of Entrepreneurial Behavior & Research*, *29*(2), 385–407.

Baker, T., Gedajlovic, E., Lubatkin, M. (2005). A framework for comparing entrepreneurship processes across nations. *Journal of International Business Studies*, *36*(5), 492–504.

Baker, T., Nelson, R. E. (2005). Creating something from nothing: resource construction through entrepreneurial bricolage. *Administrative Science Quarterly*, *50*(3), 329–366.

Barnes, W., Gartland, M., Stack, M. (2004). Old habits die hard: path dependency and behavioral lock-in. *Journal of Economic Issues*, *28*(2), 371–377.

Baron, R. A. (2007). Behavioral and cognitive factors in entrepreneurship: entrepreneurs as the active element in new venture creation. *Strategic Entrepreneurship Journal*, *1*(1–2), 167–182.

Baron, R. A. (2024). Importing knowledge from psychology: how it broadens the scope of entrepreneurship research and helps it avoid the multi-tower effect. *Small Business Economics*, *63*(4), 1355–1363.

Baron, R. A., Henry, R. A. (2011). Entrepreneurship: the genesis of organizations. In S. Zedeck (Ed.), *APA Handbook of Industrial and Organizational Psychology, Vol. 1. Building and Developing the Organization* (pp. 241–273). American Psychological Association, Washington, DC.

Bennett, V. M., Chatterji, A. K. (2023). The entrepreneurial process: evidence from a nationally representative survey. *Strategic Management Journal*, *44*(1), 86–116.

Bhave, M. P. (1994). A process model of entrepreneurial venture creation. *Journal of Business Venturing*, *9*(3), 223–242.

Boccardelli, P., Magnusson, M. G. (2006). Dynamic capabilities in early-phase entrepreneurship. *Knowledge and Process Management*, *13*(3), 162–174.

Bowman, C., Swart, J. (2007). Whose human capital? The challenge of value capture when capital is embedded. *Journal of Management Studies*, *44*(4), 488–505.

Bryan, K. A., Ryall, M. D., Schipper, B. C. (2022). Value capture in the face of known and unknown unknowns. *Strategy Science*, *7*(3), 157–189.

Bygrave, B. (2004). The entrepreneurial process. In W. Bygrave, A. E. Zacharkis (Eds.), *The Portable MBA in Entrepreneurship* (pp. 1–28). John Wiley & Sons, Hoboken, NJ.

Cohen, W. M., Levinthal, D. A. (1990). Absorptive capacity: a new perspective on learning and innovation. *Administrative Science Quarterly*, *35*(1), 128–152.

Companys, Y. E., McMullen, J. S. (2007). Strategic entrepreneurs at work: the nature, discovery, and exploitation of entrepreneurial opportunities. *Small Business Economics*, *28*(4), 301–322.

Cooper, A. C., Woo, C. A., Dunkelberg, W. (1989). Entrepreneurship and the initial size of firms. *Journal of Business Venturing*, *4*(5), 317–332.

Corbett, A. C. (2005). Experiential learning within the process of opportunity identification and exploitation. *Entrepreneurship Theory and Practice*, *29*(3), 473–491.

Corley, K. G., Gioia, D. A. (2011). Building theory about theory building: what constitutes a theoretical contribution? *The Academy of Management Review*, *36*(1), 12–32.

Covin, J. G., Slevin, D. P. (1991). A conceptual model of entrepreneurship as firm behaviour. *Entrepreneurship Theory and Practice*, *16*(1), 7–26.

Crespo, J., Suire, R., Vicente, J. (2014). Lock-in or lock-out? How structural properties of knowledge networks affect regional resilience. *Journal of Economic Geography*, *14*(1), 199–219.

Cunneen, D. J., Mankelow, G. J., Gibson, B. (2007). Towards a process model of independent growth firm creation. *Small Enterprise Research*, *15*(1), 90–105.

David, P. A. (1985). Clio and the economics of QWERTY. *The American Economic Review*, *75*(2), 332–337.

David, P. A. (2000). Path-dependence, its critics and the quest for historical economics. In P. Garrouste, S. Ioannides (Eds.), *Evolution and Path Dependence in Economic Ideas: Past and Present* (pp. 15–40). Edward Elgar Publishing, Cheltenham.

Davidsson, P., Gruenhagen, J. H. (2021). Fulfilling the process promise: a review and agenda for new venture creation process research. *Entrepreneurship Theory and Practice*, *45*(5), 1083–1118.

Dimov, D. (2018). Uncertainty under entrepreneurship. In A. Fayolle, S. Ramoglou, M. Karatas-Ozkan, K. Nicolopoulou (Eds.), *Philosophical Reflexivity and Entrepreneurship Research* (pp. 184–196). Routledge, London.

Downey, H. K., Slocum, J. W. (1975). Uncertainty: measures, research, and sources of variation. *Academy of Management Journal*, *18*(3), 562–578.

Duncan, R. B. (1972). Characteristics of organizational environments and perceived environmental uncertainty. *Administrative Science Quarterly*, *17*(3), 313–327.

Eckhardt, J. T., Ciuchta, M. P. (2008). Selected variation: the population-level implications of multistage selection in entrepreneurship. *Strategic Entrepreneurship Journal*, *2*(3), 209–224.

Eckhardt, J. T., Shane, S., Delmar, F. (2006). Multistage selection and the funding of new ventures. *Management Science*, *52*(2), 220–232.

Fayolle, A. (2007). *Entrepreneurship and New Value Creation: The Dynamic of the Entrepreneurial Process*. Cambridge University Press, Cambridge.

Gaddefors, J., Anderson, A. R. (2017). Entrepreneurship and context: when entrepreneurship is greater than entrepreneurs. *International Journal of Entrepreneurial Behavior & Research*, *23*(2), 267–278.

Gielnik, M. M., Spitzmuller, M., Schmitt, A., Klemann, D. K., Frese, M. (2015). I put in effort, therefore I am passionate: investigating the path from effort to passion in entrepreneurship. *Academy of Management Journal*, *58*(4), 1012–1031.

Gieure, C., del Mar Benavides-Espinosa, M., Roig-Dobón, S. (2020). The entrepreneurial process: the link between intentions and behavior. *Journal of Business Research*, *112*, 541–548.

Gifford, S. (2005). Risk and uncertainty. In Z. J. Acs, D. B. Audretsch (Eds.), *Handbook of Entrepreneurship Research: An Interdisciplinary Survey and Introduction* (pp. 37–53). Springer, New York.

Guerrero, M., Liñán, F., Cáceres-Carrasco, F. R. (2021). The influence of ecosystems on the entrepreneurship process: a comparison across developed and developing economies. *Small Business Economics*, *57*(4), 1733–1759.

Haber, S., Reichel, A. (2007). The cumulative nature of the entrepreneurial process: the contribution of human capital, planning and environment resources to small venture performance. *Journal of Business Venturing*, *22*(1), 119–145.

Hansen, B. (2018). Preaching to Seneca: Christ as Stoic sapiens in Divinae Institutiones IV. *Harvard Theological Review*, *111*(4), 541–558.

Heinonen, J., Poikkijoki, S. A. (2006). An entrepreneurial-directed approach to entrepreneurship education: mission impossible? *Journal of Management Development*, *25*(1), 80–94.

Held, L., Herrmann, A. M., van Mossel, A. (2018). Team formation processes in new ventures. *Small Business Economics*, *51*, 441–464.

Hmielesky, K. M., Baron, R. A. (2008). Regulatory focus and new venture performance: a study of entrepreneurial opportunity exploitation under conditions of risk versus uncertainty. *Strategic Entrepreneurship Journal*, *2*(4), 285–299.

Hornsby, J. S., Naffziger, D. W., Kuratko, D. F., Montagno, R. V. (1993). An interactive model of the corporate entrepreneurship process. *Entrepreneurship Theory and Practice*, *17*(2), 29–37.

Ireland, R. D., Hitt, M. A., Camp, S. M., Sexton, D. L. (2001). Integrating entrepreneurship and strategic management actions to create firm wealth. *Academy of Management Executive*, *15*(1), 49–63.

Jones, M. V., Coviello, N. E. (2005). Internationalisation: conceptualising an entrepreneurial process of behaviour in time. *Journal of International Business Studies*, *36*(3), 284–303.

Khilstrom, R., Laffont, J. (1979). A general equilibrium entrepreneurial theory of firm formation based on risk aversion. *Journal of Political Economy*, *87*(4), 719–748.

Knight, F. H. (1921). *Risk, Uncertainty and Profit*. August M. Kelley, New York.

Kuratko, D. F., Hornsby, J. S., Goldsby, M. G. (2007). The relationship of stakeholder salience, organizational posture, and entrepreneurial intensity to corporate entrepreneurship. *Journal of Leadership & Organizational Studies*, *13*(4), 56–72.

Lawrence, P. R., Lorsch, J. W. (1967) *Organization and Environment*. Harvard University Press, Boston, MA.

Lévesque, M., Stephan, U. (2020). It's time we talk about time in entrepreneurship. *Entrepreneurship Theory and Practice*, *44*(2), 163–184.

Leyden, D. P., Link, A. N. (2015). Toward a theory of the entrepreneurial process. *Small Business Economics*, *44*(3), 475–484.

Loch, C. H., Solt, M. E., Bailey, E. M. (2008). Diagnosing unforeseeable uncertainty in a new venture. *Journal of Product Innovation Management*, *25*(1), 28–46.

Long, C. P. (2002). The ontological reappropriation of phronēsis. *Continental Philosophy Review*, *35*(1), 35–60.

Lyu, J., Shepherd, D., Lee, K. (2024). The impact of entrepreneurship pedagogy on nascent student entrepreneurship: an entrepreneurial process perspective. *Studies in Higher Education*, *49*(1), 62–83.

Matricano, D. (2015). *Lo Studio dell'Imprenditorialità. Un Approccio di Indagine Multidimensionale*. Carocci Editore, Roma.

Matricano, D. (2023). *Interdisciplinarity in Entrepreneurship: Investigating Issues and Debates with New Lenses*. Springer Nature, Cham.

Matricano, D. (2024). Entrepreneurship: shaping the future | the manifesto. *International Entrepreneruship and Management Journal*, *20*(4), 3113–3123.

Matricano, D. (2025a). Dynamic capabilities in entrepreneurship—DyCE: a new domain for theoretical and empirical research. *Journal of Small Business Management*. https://doi.org/10.1080/00472778.2025.2503372

Matricano, D. (2025b). Dynamic capabilities in entrepreneurship. In J. Mitra (Ed.), *The Palgrave Encyclopedia of Entrepreneurship* (pp. 1–5). Palgrave Macmillan, Cham.

McDonald, F. (2025). Entrepreneurial posture and its strategic impact on business success and growth. *European International Journal of Multidisciplinary Research and Management Studies*, *5*(5), 1–6.

Moreno-Gata, S., Rodríguez-Torres, R., Betancor, V., Rodríguez-Pérez, A. (2024). Humanizing the transgressor and lightening the immoral behavior: the role of likeability bias and moral rationalization. *Behavioral Sciences*, *14*(12), 1–17.

Moroz, P. W., Hindle, K. (2012). Entrepreneurship as a process: toward harmonizing multiple perspectives. *Entrepreneurship Theory and Practice*, *36*(4), 781–818.

Morrissey, P. (2012). The sapiential dimension of theology according to St. Thomas. *New Blackfriars*, *93*(1045), 309–323.

Neergaard, H., Robinson, S., Jones, S. (2021). Transformative learning in the entrepreneurship education process: the role of pedagogical nudging and reflection. *International Journal of Entrepreneurial Behavior & Research*, *27*(1), 251–277.

Okhuysen, G., Bonardi, J. P. (2011). The challenges of building theory by combining lenses. *Academy of Management Review*, *36*(1), 6–11.

Parker, S. C. (2006). Learning about the unknown: how fast do entrepreneurs adjust their beliefs? *Journal of Business Venturing*, *21*(1), 1–26.

Pinto, J. K., Patanakul, P., Pinto, M. B. (2015). Gender biases in hiring project managers: perceptions of trust and likeability. *IEEE Transactions on Engineering Management*, *62*(3), 325–334.

Rorty, A. O. (1978). The place of contemplation in Aristotle's Nicomachean Ethics. *Mind*, *87*(347), 343–358.

Ruef, M. (2005). Origins of organizations: the entrepreneurial process. In L. A. Keister (Ed.), *Entrepreneurship. Research in the Sociology of Work* (Vol. 15, pp. 63–100). Emerald Group Publishing Limited, Bingley.

Santoso, A. S., Soh, P. H., Larso, D., Chen, J. (2020). Strategic entrepreneurship in a VUCA environment: perspectives from Asian emerging economies. *International Journal of Entrepreneurial Venturing*, *12*(4), 343–354.

Sarasvathy, S. D., Dew, N., Velamuri, S. R., Venkataraman, S. (2005). Three views of entrepreneurial opportunity. In Z. J. Acs, D. B. Audretsch (Eds.), *Handbook of Entrepreneurship Research: An Interdisciplinary Survey and Introduction* (pp. 77–96). Springer, New York.

Scheibel, O., Osiyevskyy, O., Radnejad, A. B. (2025). Strategic entrepreneurship in VUCA environment: the competing forces of outcome variability. *Management Research Review*, *48*(2), 214–230.

Shane, S. (2003). *A General Theory of Entrepreneurship. The Individual-Opportunity Nexus*. Edward Elgar Publishing, Cheltenham.

Shane, S., Venkataraman, S. (2000). The promise of entrepreneurship as a field of research. *Academy of Management Review*, *25*(1), 217–226.

Sleptsov, A., Anand, J. (2008). Exercising entrepreneurial opportunities: the role of information-gathering and information-processing capabilities of the firm. *Strategic Entrepreneurship Journal*, *2*(4), 357–372.

Slotte-Kock, S., Coviello, N. (2010). Entrepreneurship research on network processes: a review and ways forward. *Entrepreneurship Theory and Practice*, *34*(1), 31–57.

Small, M. W. (2013). Business practice, ethics and the philosophy of morals in the Rome of Marcus Tullius Cicero. *Journal of Business Ethics*, *115*(2), 341–350.

Steyaert, C. (2007). Entrepreneuring as a conceptual attractor? A review of process theories in 20 years of entrepreneurship studies. *Entrepreneurship and Regional Development*, *19*(6), 453–477.

Teece, D. J. (2023). The evolution of the dynamic capabilities framework. In R. Adams, D. Grichnik, A. Pundziene, C. Volkmann (Eds.), *Artificiality and Sustainability in Entrepreneurship. Studies in Small Business and Entrepreneurship* (pp. 113–129). Springer, Cham.

Teece, D. J., Pisano, G., Shuen, A. (1997). Dynamic capabilities and strategic management. *Strategic Management Journal*, *18*(7), 509–533.

Thoumrungroje, A., Tansuhaj, P. (2005). Entrepreneurial strategic posture, international diversification, and firm performance. *Multinational Business Review*, *13*(1), 55–73.

Townsend, D. M., Hunt, R. A., McMullen, J. S., Sarasvathy, S. D. (2018). Uncertainty, knowledge problems, and entrepreneurial action. *Academy of Management Annals*, *12*(2), 659–687.

Ucbasaran, D., Westhead, P., Wright, M. (2008). Opportunity identification and pursuit, does an entrepreneur's human capital matter? *Small Business Economics*, *30*(2), 153–173.

Wang, C., Dai, M., Fang, Y., Liu, C. (2022). Ideas and methods of lean and agile startup in the VUCA Era. *International Entrepreneurship and Management Journal*, *18*(4), 1527–1544.

Welter, F. (2011). Contextualizing entrepreneurship – conceptual challenges and ways forward. *Entrepreneurship Theory and Practice*, *35*(1), 165–184.

Williams, R. (1990). Sapientia and the trinity reflections on the De Trinitate. *Augustiniana*, *40*(1/4), 317–332.

Williams, T. A., Li, J. M., Zhao, E. Y. (2024). Entrepreneurial resourcefulness: theoretical origins, integrative review, and research agenda. *Journal of Management Studies*. https://doi.org/10.1111/joms.13181

Winkler, C., Fust, A., Jenert, T. (2023). From entrepreneurial experience to expertise: a self-regulated learning perspective. *Journal of Small Business Management*, *61*(4), 2071–2096.

Wood, G., Pereira, V., Temouri, Y., Wilkinson, A. (2021). Exploring and investigating sustainable international business practices by MNEs in emerging markets. *International Business Review*, *30*(5), 101899.

Zahra, S. A., Sapienza, H. J., Davidsson, P. (2006). Entrepreneurship and dynamic capabilities: a review, model and research agenda. *Journal of Management Studies*, *43*(4), 917–955.

4 The Harmonic Entrepreneur

Mariacarmela Passarelli

4.1 The genesis of the concept of the Harmonic Entrepreneur

In a very complex economic and social world, the idea of the Harmonic Entrepreneur responds to the urgent challenge for entrepreneurs to connect *who* they are (identity and value) with *what* and *how* they do (decisions, actions, relationships) (Gregori, 2024; Steyaert, 2007). Classical economic thought paid limited and often indirect attention to the nature of the entrepreneur. Ricardo (1817) almost ignored the role, while Smith (1776) merged entrepreneur, capitalist, and manager into a single role, driven by self-interest and coordinated by the "invisible hand" (Baron & Shane, 2007; Bennett & Chatterji, 2023; Moroz & Hindle, 2012; Audretsch, 2012; Eckhardt & Shane, 2003; Krueger et al., 2000; Shane, 2003; Denicolai et al., 2015; Kuratko et al., 2015; Munoz & Dimov, 2023; Ranfagni & Runfola, 2018; European Commission, 2021). Cantillon (1756) offers the first definition of 'entrepreneur' as a key figure in economic self-regulation, someone who bears risk, competes, and adjusts to market signals and thus laid the foundation for modern economic models. Cantillon's entrepreneur was not merely a government contractor but a market agent whose role was essential for the proper functioning of the economy. This self-regulating role of entrepreneurs mirrors Isaac Newton's concept of gravity regulating the physical world, and Cantillon's work can be seen as applying similar principles to the economy. Say (1861) separated the capitalist/owner from the entrepreneur, who organizes, directs, and combines resources creatively. Marshall, in his *Principles of Economics* (1890), held land, labour, capital, and organization to be the four factors of production and considered entrepreneurship as the driving factor that brings these four factors together. Overall, the classical tradition portrayed the entrepreneur/capitalist as a *homo faber/homo economicus*, guided primarily by instrumental rationality and profit maximization. However, the classical approach is incomplete; in fact, it ignores other dimensions that inform entrepreneurial choice. In the view of the Austrian school, the entrepreneur took on a totally dynamic and central attractive role in economic development. Schumpeter (1934) (Austrian School) in

DOI: 10.4324/9781003681182-4

fact developed a theory in which the defining function of the entrepreneur is innovation: 'doing new things or doing old things in a new way'; this new view interprets the entrepreneur as a creative force who introduces new combinations of resources, generating 'creative destruction' that breaks the existing equilibrium and generates development. In this perspective, the aim is not only profit but also the transformation of the economic system and the creation of new value. In 1973, Kirzner's *Competition and Entrepreneurship* (Neo-Austrian School) introduced the concept of alertness that reinforces the 'proactive' attitude of entrepreneurship, defining the entrepreneur as an intermediary who discovers and exploits market opportunities. According to Kirzner (2009), in fact, it is always possible to say that by 'seeing' the opportunity, the entrepreneur actually creates it. Drucker (1985) offers a new perspective, by explicitly rejecting the cognitive and psychological approach to entrepreneurship that characterizes the (neo-) Austrian School, Drucker (1985) argues that 'the entrepreneur always seeks change, responds to it, and exploits it as an opportunity', by giving to the entrepreneur the function of introducing or doing new things in a new way. This definition represents a crucial point since it preserves the centrality of change and opportunity-seeking but transforms entrepreneurship from a discovery function driven by alertness (Kirzner) into a strategic vision that translates the idea into practice and results.

However, the literature also proposes a broader vision that can combine different individual characteristics with the entrepreneurial role (Mmbaga et al., 2020; Radu-Lefebvre et al., 2021). According to the discovery theory (Alvarez & Barney, 2007), in fact, the entrepreneur's role lies primarily in identifying opportunities that exist objectively, typically arising from exogenous changes in markets, technologies, or regulation. By contrast, the creation theory holds that opportunities do not pre-exist; they are endogenously brought into being through entrepreneurs' iterative actions, exploring new scenarios, experimenting with methods, and developing novel products and services. From this creation perspective, the centrality of the entrepreneur's personal traits and decision-making capabilities becomes especially salient. The theory of opportunity creation emphasizes the entrepreneur's creativity, their ability to apply their intelligence to a problem of any nature that leads to a solution that is new compared to the past, based on the available knowledge and the ability to combine forms of divergent and convergent, lateral and vertical, outside and inside the box thinking (Baccarani, 2010). Thus, an objective dimension can be attributed to opportunities while recognizing that they cannot emerge and materialize without the role of certain individuals: the entrepreneurs. Accordingly, as Publius Terentius Afer, argues in his comedy *Heautontimorumenos* (The Self-Punisher, v. 77), as early as 165 BC, stated: "Homo sum, humani nihil a me alienum puto" (*I am a man, and everything human concerns me*).

Consistent with this view, being an entrepreneur is a human and professional life experience. Rather than a purely rational utility-maximizer, in fact, the entrepreneur can be seen as an affective, relational agent, *homo economicus* as well as *homo sentimentalis*, who acts, interacts, and constructs meaning through situated practices, processes, and contexts (Gregori, 2024; Steyaert, 2007).

The Tragedy of the Commons by Garrett Hardin (1968) offers a powerful metaphor for the tension between individual interest and collective well-being. The meadow is very large but not large enough to accommodate an infinite number of animals. Therefore, each shepherd should refrain from expanding his flock. For the shepherd's individual interest, an additional sheep would mean greater profit, but for the common good, having more animals would mean exhausting the resources that sustain them sooner. Each shepherd, therefore, must necessarily give up a portion of personal gain (in the short term) to protect collective gain (in the long term).

This story brings us back to thinking about other aspects that can be considered, and a necessity of a caring perspective emerges (André & Pache, 2016; Gallo & Melé, 2025; Rodriguez et al., 2025). While traditional entrepreneurship is based on the profitable discovery and exploitation of opportunities, the 'entrepreneurship of care' leans on human dignity and on the social mission, utilizing economic success as a means rather than an end. It emphasizes the value of relationships and dependencies in human life, proposing ethical behaviour based on empathy, compassion, and concern for the needs of people (Linsley, 2017); it encourages caring relationships among members and develop the capacity to listen to different voices (André & Pache, 2016); moreover, it integrates justice, care, and virtues as contents of person-centred ethics (Melé, 2024). Within this perspective, some researchers also propose the inclusion of People With Mental Illness and/or Intellectual Disability (PWMI/ID) (Mzembe & Filimonau, 2024). Thus, the entrepreneurship of care prioritizes the human need and the person's fulfilment, adapting organizational structures to people rather than people to structures. The mercantile humanism of Benedetto Cotrugli (1458) reminds us that there is no ethical business without people of sound principles. This approach, in fact, has its roots in the ethics of virtues (Aristotle), and it traces harmony back to *eudemonia*, the 'good life' that springs from just and temperate actions and also values *philautia*, well-ordered self-love, as a condition for loving others. The tradition of *humanitas* (by Terence) insists on dignity, reciprocity, and civil bonds, while the social doctrine (e.g., Laborem Exercens, Laudato si', Caritas in veritate) and the Biblical references (Genesis, Exodus, Gospels) refer to free will, responsibility, and the vocation to put talents at the service of the common good.

According to this perspective, entrepreneurs cannot confine their action to a purely utilitarian view of entrepreneurship. Instead, they place the human being (themselves and all stakeholders) at the centre of entrepreneurial attention, seeking to harmonize and reconcile responsibility toward themselves, people, communities, and future generations with business objectives.

4.2 From harmony to harmonic

Entrepreneur as *homo sentimentalis* works on the 'harmonization' of heterogeneous objectives: economics, sociality, or environmental (Coda, 2020). In fact, in a world that is volatile, uncertain, complex, and ambiguous, VUCA (Scheibel et al., 2025; Wang et al., 2022), the true challenge of every entrepreneur is to hold different parts together in a coherent whole: this is the essence of harmony. The term derives from the Greek harmonía (ἁρμονία), which means 'joint', 'agreement', 'good fit'. Harmonia, in fact, is the Greek goddess of harmony and the daughter of Ares (god of war) and Aphrodite (goddess of love and beauty), who tried to bring together opposing forces. With Aristotle, harmony meets the ethics of *mesótes*, the measure that avoids excesses and defects. The Roman world and Stoicism transform harmony into civil bond (concordia), while Christian thought brings it back to order and beauty. In the Middle Ages and the Renaissance, harmony guided the arts and sciences: from polyphony to proportional architecture, to Kepler's search for celestial harmonies. Between the modern and contemporary ages, 'harmonic' entered into the life and social sciences and harmony became a powerful metaphor for describing complex systems in which autonomous parts cooperate, correct each other, and adapt. Thus, translated into entrepreneurship, harmony means first and foremost the capacity to work through and creatively resolve tensions, starting from the tension between profit and value (economic, social, and environmental). In fact, in a changing world characterized by grand societal challenges, rapid technological transformation, and the growing interdependence of economic, social, and ecological systems, it is necessary to integrate individual identity and persona values with environmental needs and perspectives (Cicione, 2023; Passarelli, 2024). Coherently, 'harmony' refers to a way of designing and governing a business that recognizes a plurality of goals and constraints. Thus, inner harmony enables individuals to perceive different opportunities with lucidity and to evaluate them with integrity. Through attentive listening and observation, these opportunities are exploited by orchestrating knowledge, capital, and processes to innovate, while reconciling the pursuit of the new with care for what must be preserved, above all relationships and nature.

4.3 The characteristics of the Harmonic Entrepreneur: a three-pronged diamond

Who is the Harmonic Entrepreneur, what do they do and how? In line with the seminal definition (Passarelli, 2024), the Harmonic Entrepreneurs are defined as 'three-pronged diamonds'. These individuals are proactive beings who, with responsibility, must take care of themselves and what surrounds them, finding a meeting point between individual respect, collective respect, and respect for creation. The three main beliefs that represent harmonic entrepreneurship are as follows: *Salus salutis* (harmony with oneself that is self-care and personal well-being); *Homo humanitas* (harmony in relationships that is caring for people and the common good); and *Homo humus* (harmony with creation, with a correct relationship with the goods of the world and the *patermunus*). The Harmonic Entrepreneur lives in harmony with themselves, with others, and with creation.

The care of oneself is an obvious precondition for taking care of the business and people other than oneself. This principle focuses on personal well-being, defined as the individual's physical and psychological health (Shepherd & Patzelt, 2011; Wiklund et al., 2017). The word 'health' derives from the Latin *'salus, salutis'*, meaning 'safety, soundness, integrity, health', akin to *'salvus'* meaning 'safe'. The World Health Organization (WHO) has redefined health not merely as the absence of disease but as "the ability to adapt and self-manage in the face of social, physical, and emotional challenges" (OMS, 2011).

Entrepreneurship can be likened to an 'emotional roller coaster', involving intense positive feelings (like happiness and fun) and negative feelings (like anger and stress) (Bencsik & Chuluun, 2021; Cardon et al., 2012; McEwen, 2004). Entrepreneurs are susceptible to stress and often blur the boundary between their lives and the company, perceiving business failures as personal failures. The desire for success and the extreme sense of duty often lead the entrepreneur to 'work too much', dedicating more hours than other professionals, which impacts physiological and mental balance. Entrepreneurs, in fact, are always under pressure and they must continuously react to recognize and exploit opportunities. Decisions involve the human brain (Waldman et al., 2016) and have a connection with some well-known concepts in neuroscience (Massaro et al., 2023; Mehta & Josephs, 2010; Mehta et al., 2015). In the entrepreneurial literature, there are several studies that analyse the relationship between neuroscience and its effect on specific entrepreneurial variables (Mehta & Josephs, 2010; Mehta et al., 2015), such as the identification of entrepreneurial opportunities (Nicolaou & Shane, 2009, 2014) and entrepreneurial alertness (Cucino et al., 2022). Considering these new study perspectives, the results of research analysing the importance of biological factors on entrepreneurship can become a useful tool to help entrepreneurs regain harmony with their body and mind, improving their state of health.

Thus, the seeds of entrepreneurial activity are inevitably tied to the identity and to the sentiments of individual actors and also to the ability to restore harmony and ethics towards oneself. The love of self (*philautìa*, according to Aristotle), in fact, is viewed as a sacred duty and a tool for achieving the happiness of the collective. Thus, the Harmonic Entrepreneurs must use their 'oxygen mask', adopting a lifestyle that supports self-care and reduces anxiety and stress, improving the ability to navigate through the entrepreneurial process. Consequently, these principles focus on the capacity to establish genuinely human and fraternal relationships in all spheres of life. Since the entrepreneur is an economic agent, but first and foremost is a social and sentimental actor, when interacting with stakeholders the entrepreneur must deploy a series of skills that involve the emotional sphere that includes emotional intelligence as a driver for growth and harmonious innovation (Deng et al., 2023) and the attitude of kindness and motivation to generate positive relationships (Melo & Anderson, 2016).

This perspective builds on the classical concept of philanthropy, understood as respect for all human beings, and on Cicero's notion of *humanitas* as an objective moral principle. It conceives the entrepreneur as someone who is open to diversity and accustomed to inclusion, actively seeking to valorize the talent and potential of marginalized groups (e.g., persons with disabilities, migrants) (Meng & Kim, 2025). Thus, the Harmonic Entrepreneurs is a builder of positive interpersonal relationships.

Moreover, the Harmonic Entrepreneur promotes the "humanisation of science and technologies" (Sanguedolce et al., 2025), that is, a mode of scientific and technological development oriented toward human needs, conducted ethically, and respectful of everyone's rights. In fact, technology should not be an end in itself, but rather a primary enabler of innovation that produces tangible benefits through collaboration between humans and machines. Moreover, the Harmonic Entrepreneurs support a model of production and consumption based on sharing, reuse, repair, and recycling, extending the life cycle of products and minimizing waste; this contrasts with the traditional linear economic model ('extract, produce, use, and discard') (Shepherd & Patzelt, 2017). The Harmonic Entrepreneur's commitment to the planet, in fact, aligns with global frameworks like the UN Agenda 2030 and the European Commission's New Green Deal. Caring for creation entails embracing a logic of gratuitousness, love, and service rather than domination. In this view, scientific and technological progress should serve the good of all humanity, rather than produce inequalities or encourage the destructive exploitation of human and natural resources. Accordingly, the Harmonic Entrepreneur emerges not only as an innovator, but also as a mindful custodian of creation, respectful of nature's rhythms and biodiversity (Vlasov, 2021).

For the Harmonic Entrepreneur, opportunities are seen not only as pre-existing 'gaps in the market' to be exploited for profit but as possibilities for enhancing human well-being and dignity. In this sense, opportunities are interpreted and constructed through an anthropocentric lens: they emerge from the recognition of unmet human needs, inequalities, and latent capabilities, especially those of marginalized groups, and are evaluated according to their potential to generate both economic value and common good. Thus, the Harmonic Entrepreneurs engage with opportunities as occasions to humanize technologies, empower people, and foster inclusive development, rather than merely as vehicles for financial gain (Sarason et al., 2006). After having outlined the characteristics of the Harmonic Entrepreneurs, we now consider how they actually pass through the entrepreneurial processes.

4.4 A harmonic navigation through the entrepreneurial process

The Harmonic Entrepreneur adopts Shane and Venkataraman's (2000) view of entrepreneurship as a process of opportunity identification, evaluation, and exploitation because it explicitly focuses on a double nexus (individual-opportunity and individual-context) (Brown et al., 2024; Dimov, 2002; Fortunato & Alter, 2011; Sarason et al., 2006; Shane and Eckhardt, 2003).

In line with this theoretical framework, the Harmonic Entrepreneur is inspired by the interaction of two main drivers: to be well (personal well-being) (Diener, 1984, 1994; Kahneman et al., 1999; Ryff & Singer, 2008; Stephan et al., 2023) and to exist well (entrepreneurship of care) (Harris et al., 2009; Miles et al., 2004; Vallaster et al., 2019). Since the concept of the Harmonic Entrepreneur is anthropocentric, by putting the human being at the core of every entrepreneurial decision, well-being functions as both a design principle and an evaluative standard, structuring how opportunities are discovered, evaluated, and exploited (André & Pache, 2016; De Cuyper et al., 2024; Stephan et al., 2023) by promoting an idiosyncratic, context-embedded individual.

Specifically, in the discovery phase, the concept of 'to be well' inspires the balance of mental, physical, and emotional well-being that sustains the clarity, attention, and cognitive openness needed to recognize entrepreneurial opportunities. Self-care (*philautìa*), in fact, supports sustained attention, listening, and observation, and the entrepreneur manages the emotional roller coaster, cultivates optimism and passion, and avoids forms of stress or burnout that blur perception. The discovery is led by an ethic of care from an entrepreneur with the attitude to seize opportunities that can 'generate good', not only profit. Through 'feeling' and listening to people and communities, the Harmonic Entrepreneur recognizes problems where entrepreneurial action can make a positive social and environmental impact (relationships, nature, stakeholders). The discovery of opportunities is also driven by the concept of "to exist well", which helps to orient perception toward problems whose resolution can generate positive social and environmental impact from the perspective of the entrepreneurship of care.

The evaluation phase is affected by the impact of opportunities on personal physical and psychological health (workload, stress, lifestyle). In fact, opportunities that structurally compromise inner harmony (e.g., chronic overload, toxic environments) are discarded. During the evaluation phase, the Harmonic Entrepreneur does not limit the analysis to risk–return calculations or competitive positioning. Rather, the assessment of an opportunity is explicitly filtered through ethical and societal lenses. The entrepreneur pauses to ask: will this opportunity contribute to the common good?, that is to say: will it enhance people's well-being, respect their rights, reduce inequalities, or empower marginalized groups? This question acts as a normative compass that can lead to the redefinition, reshaping, or even rejection of opportunities that, although profitable, would generate social or environmental harm. In this way, ethical and societal values do not represent an 'add-on' ex post but become core criteria that structure how opportunities are weighed, prioritized, and ultimately pursued. Thus, *Homo humanitas and Homo humus* are part of the value assessment, and financial success must serve a larger purpose and cannot be the sole driver. In the exploitation phase, the Harmonic Entrepreneur orchestrates knowledge, capital, and processes not only to capture economic value but to make resources available to others, designing work and leadership practices inspired by empathy, solidarity, legality, and gratitude, and conceiving the enterprise as a communal entity whose financial success must serve a broader purpose. Exploitation is conceived as entrepreneurship of care, and the resources are mobilized to enable others to exist well. Thus, the exploitation of opportunity goes hand in hand with the growth of people, the quality of work, and the care of creation. In this perspective, the enterprise is seen as a communal entity where customers receive fair value, collaborators reach an adequate standard of living, communities benefit from responsible resource use; thus, leadership is inspired by empathy, solidarity, mercy, legality, and gratitude.

Across the entrepreneurial process, each step is interpreted not only in economic terms but also in terms of health, happiness, and social impact, which reinforce a virtuous cycle of "being well in order to generate good" through subsequent opportunity discovery, evaluation, and exploitation. See Table 4.1.

From this analysis emerges not only a clear nexus between individuals and opportunity but also the nexus between the individuals and the contexts (Sarason et al., 2006). In summary, the Harmonic Entrepreneur does not follow a different entrepreneurial process from other entrepreneurs; however, the approach to decision-making across the entrepreneurial process is different, because as a human being, the Harmonic Entrepreneur attempts to create harmony among heterogeneous factors. For this reason, it is interesting to shift the attention to the analysis of the decisional mechanisms in order to identify the peculiarities of the Harmonic Entrepreneur across the process.

4.5 Making harmonic decisions: the emerging role of the Harmonic Entrepreneurs

The characteristics of the Harmonic Entrepreneurs are consistent with a view of the entrepreneur as *homo sentimentalis*, who co-evolves with both opportunities and the contexts in which they are embedded (Illouz, 2007; Sarason et al., 2006; Shane & Venkataraman, 2000; Steyaert, 2007). Accordingly, entrepreneurial decision-making emerges from the interplay between this double nexus (individual-opportunity and individual-context) and from the heterogeneity of both individuals and their opportunity–context configurations (Shepherd et al., 2015).

Table 4.1 The Harmonic Entrepreneur across the entrepreneurial process

Shane and Venkataraman's entrepreneurial process (2000)	*The Harmonic Entrepreneur*	*The Harmonic Entrepreneur*
	"to be well"	*"to exist well"*
	(salus salutis)	(Homo humanitas and Homo humus)
Opportunity discovery	Harmony (mental, physical, emotional well-being) enables clarity in perceiving 'reality' and future scenario to identify opportunities. The entrepreneur manages the emotional roller coaster, cultivates optimism and passion, and avoids forms of stress or burnout that blur perception. Self-care (philautìa) supports sustained attention, listening, and observation.	Discovery is guided by an ethic of care: the Harmonic Entrepreneur has the posture to catch opportunities that can 'generate good', not only profit. Through 'feeling' and listening to people and communities, the Harmonic Entrepreneur recognizes problems where entrepreneurial action can produce positive social and environmental impact (relationships, nature, and stakeholders).
Opportunity evaluation	The Harmonic Entrepreneur considers the impact on personal physical and psychological health (workload, stress, lifestyle). Coherence between what one thinks, says, and does (eudaimonia) becomes a key evaluation criterion. Opportunities that structurally compromise inner harmony (e.g., chronic overload, toxic environments) are discarded.	Evaluation includes ethical and societal value: "Will this opportunity contribute to the common good?" The Harmonic Entrepreneur weighs not only economic outcomes but also social impact, respect for legality, fairness, and environmental sustainability. *Homo humanitas* (relationships) and *Homo humus* (creation) is part of the value assessment. Financial success must serve a larger purpose and cannot be the sole driver.
Opportunity exploitation	In exploiting the opportunity, the Harmonic Entrepreneur orchestrates knowledge, capital, and processes in a way that supports both performance and health (*mens sana in corpore sano*). They design routines of self-care (movement, exercise, rest, emotional regulation) and a work organization that reduces stress and burnout, fostering positive emotions, creativity, and passion for work.	Exploitation is conceived as entrepreneurship of care: resources are mobilized to enable others to 'exist well'. The enterprise is seen as a communal entity: customers receive fair value, collaborators reach an adequate standard of living, communities benefit from responsible resource use. Leadership is inspired by empathy, solidarity, mercy, legality, and gratitude; the Harmonic Entrepreneur "exists well" by acting for durable, purpose-aligned results.

Source: Author's personal elaboration.

As Shepherd et al. (2015) argue, entrepreneurs differ in their human capital (knowledge, skills, prior experiences), and these differences shape how they search for, interpret, and pursue opportunities. They are also heterogeneous in their emotional responses to entrepreneurial opportunities as well as in how they perceive and interpret environmental conditions, including uncertainty and market dynamics. Such cognitive, emotional, and perceptual differences affect which opportunities are recognized as attractive and feasible, how risks and trade-offs are evaluated, and ultimately which entrepreneurial courses of action are chosen. Thus, the entrepreneurial process (Shane & Venkataraman, 2000) is influenced by some decision-specific factors. Within the double nexus (individual-opportunity and individual-context) (Sarason et al., 2006), entrepreneurs often perceive opportunities as mirrors of the self, interpreting them through the lens of their identity and values. Consequently, discovery, evaluation, and exploitation constantly feed back into one another, reshaping both the opportunity set and the entrepreneur. Specifically, what an entrepreneur cares about (values, motives, and past experience) tunes what they notice in the environment and the same signal can look like a great or poor opportunity depending on whether it fits one's ethics, purpose, and desired impact. Selecting and enacting an opportunity reinforces (or revises) who the entrepreneur is trying to be.

The entrepreneur is a reflexive agent engaged in purposeful action; the sources of opportunity are pre-existing features of markets, technologies, and institutions that furnish the context for venture creation. Entrepreneurship occurs as agents specify, interpret, and act upon these sources, transforming the opportunity set, even as their own beliefs, capabilities, and preferences are reshaped by the interaction. The interactive coming together of entrepreneur and opportunity is conceptualized as a duality whereby the entrepreneur and opportunity cannot exist independently and therefore cannot be understood separately and distinct from each other. Thus, each harmonic, human-centred entrepreneur and each opportunity co-evolve through repeated cycles across the entrepreneurial process where profit is necessary but not sufficient, and all the choices must also preserve well-being and generate common-good impact.

Thus, decisions are driven by harmony, coherently with the message of Pope Benedetto XVI in the Encyclical *Caritas in Veritate* (2009, p. 31): "Intelligence and love are not in separate compartments: love is rich in intelligence and intelligence is full of love". Therefore, the Harmonic Entrepreneur is someone who, in recognizing, evaluating, and realizing opportunities, integrates personal virtues and technical skills, long-term vision and executive discipline, attention to people, and respect for creation. Their success is not measured only in profits or market share, but in generating trust and social capital, together with the quality of work, care for communities, and regeneration of territories. This is not an abstract appeal to morality but a concrete proposal. Understood in this way, entrepreneurship returns to being what it can and must be: a practice of responsible freedom that creates a future on a human scale. Thus, this is a distinctive approach to entrepreneurial decision-making, one that deliberately harmonizes profit with well-being and the common good. In this view, harmony becomes a guiding design and evaluation principle throughout the entire entrepreneurial process (opportunity discovery, evaluation, and exploitation) within a co-evolving nexus among individuals, opportunities, and contexts.

4.6 Advancing a harmonic view of entrepreneurship

The profile of the Harmonic Entrepreneurs partly overlaps with previous theories, partly open new trajectories of research. The chapter attempted to clarify *who* the Harmonic Entrepreneurs are (identity and value) with *what* and *how* they do (decisions, actions, relationships) (Steyaert, 2007). The profile of the Harmonic Entrepreneur emerges as an evolution of the classical and modern model, in a context of epochal change that requires overcoming the economy based on individual interest, in order to adopt an economy founded on a sense of community and collective well-being. It converges with aspects of prior work yet forges new research paths. Specifically, the conceptual foundation of Harmonic Entrepreneur transcends the traditional utilitarian vision of entrepreneurship (Drucker, 1985), by underlining the entrepreneurship of care (André & Pache, 2016), and asks for a strong multidisciplinary convergence (Matricano, 2023; Passarelli, 2024). For the Harmonic Entrepreneur, profit is merely one of multiple objectives (competitive, economic-financial, social, and environmental) that must be harmonized. In fact, profit sought is distinguished by *how* it is pursued (based on efficiency and humanity) and *how* it is employed, favouring the long-term functionality and development of the enterprise. This approach does not pit ethics against business; rather, it advances a harmonic dialogue in which values are translated into strategic criteria, engaging all human dimensions and multiple social aspects. In doing so, it calls for a robust interdisciplinary conversation among heterogeneous, to inform and enrich entrepreneurial decision-making. In fact, economics and management offer tools for leading entrepreneurial processes and organizing means and resources (Drucker, 1985; Shane, 2000); psychology and neuroscience help us understand cognition, emotions, stress, passion, and motivations (Krueger & Welpe, 2014; Melo & Anderson, 2016; Mehta et al., 2015; Nicolaou & Shane, 2014; Nicolaou et al., 2009; Nofal & Nicolaou, 2021; Nofal et al., 2018); philosophy and ethics help to clarify the meaning of action (Miles et al., 2004; Toledano, 2022; Passarelli et al., 2025); environmental sciences remind us of planetary limits and intergenerational responsibility (De Groot & Steg, 2008; Youssef et al., 2018). A harmonic view of entrepreneurship invites a rich research agenda that is simultaneously theoretical, empirical, and normative, calling scholars to rethink what it means to create value 'for' and 'with' human beings.

The harmonic profile is not an idealized blueprint but a viable orientation for engaging human and social complexity. However, the first step is to acknowledge it and commit to moving in that direction.

References

André, K., Pache, A. C. (2016). From caring entrepreneur to caring enterprise: addressing the ethical challenges of scaling up social enterprises. *Journal of Business Ethics, 133*(4), 659–675.

Alvarez, S. A., Barney, J. B. (2007). Guest editors' introduction. The entrepreneurial theory of the firm. *Journal of Management Studies, 44*(7), 1057–1063.

Audretsch, D. (2012). Entrepreneurship research. *Management Decision, 50*(5), 755–764.

Baccarani, C. (2010). Complessità e intelligenza manageriale. *Sinergie Italian Journal of Management, 81*(10), 97–111.

Baron, R. A., Shane, S. (2007). Entrepreneurship: a process perspective. In J. R. Baum, M. Frese, R. A. Baron (Eds.), *The Psychology of Entrepreneurship* (chapter 2, pp. 19–40). Psychology Press, Taylor & Francis, Hove.

Bencsik, P., Chuluun, T. (2021). Comparative well-being of the self-employed and paid employees in the USA. *Small Business Economics, 56*(1), 355–384.

Benedetto XVI. (2009). Caritas in veritate. Libreria Editrice Vaticana.

Bennett, V. M., Chatterji, A. K. (2023). The entrepreneurial process: evidence from a nationally representative survey. *Strategic Management Journal, 44*(1), 86–116.

Brown, S., Mena, R., Brown, S. (2024). The peace dilemma in the triple nexus: challenges and opportunities for the humanitarian–development–peace approach. *Development in Practice, 34*(5), 568–584.

Cantillon, R. (1756). *Essai Sur La Nature Du Commerce En General.* Fetcher Gyler, London.

Cardon, M. S., Foo, M. D., Shepherd, D., Wiklund, J. (2012). Exploring the heart: entrepreneurial emotion is a hot topic. *Entrepreneurship Theory and Practice, 36*(1), 1–10.

Cicione, F. (2023). *Compendio di innovazione armonica.* Rubbettino, Soveria Mannelli, Italy.

Coda, V. (2020). Lo scopo dell'impresa. *Impresa Progetto, 3*, 1–26.

Cucino, V., Passarelli, M., Di Minin, A., Cariola, A. (2022). Neuroscience approach for management and entrepreneurship: a bibliometric analysis. *European Journal of Innovation Management, 25*(6), 295–319.

De Cuyper, L., Clarysse, B., Wright, M. (2024). Doing good while making profits: a typology of business models for social ventures. *Strategic Entrepreneurship Journal, 18*(2), 258–285.

De Groot, J. I., Steg, L. (2008). Value orientations to explain beliefs related to environmental significant behavior: how to measure egoistic, altruistic, and biospheric value orientations. *Environment and Behavior, 40*(3), 330–354.

Deng, X., Chen, J., Zhao, Y. (2023). Mediation effects of positive and negative affect on the relationship between emotional intelligence and life satisfaction in rural school teachers. *Frontiers in Psychology, 14*, 1129692.

Denicolai, S., Hagen, B., Pisoni, A. (2015). Be international or be innovative? Be both? The role of the entrepreneurial profile. *Journal of International Entrepreneurship, 13*(4), 390–417.

Diener, E. (1984). Subjective well-being. *Psychological Bulletin, 95*(3), 542–575.

Diener, E. (1994). Assessing subjective well-being: Progress and opportunities. *Social Indicators Research, 31*(2), 103–157.

Dimov, D. (2002). The nexus of individual and opportunity: opportunity recognition as a learning process. In *Babson College, Babson Kauffman Entrepreneurship Research*

Conference (BKERC) (Vol. 2006, pp. 410–420). Available at SSRN: https://ssrn.com/abstract=1783742.

Drucker, P. F. (1985). Entrepreneurial strategies. *California Management Review, 27*(2), 9–25.

Eckhardt, J. T., Shane, S. A. (2003). Opportunities and entrepreneurship. *Journal of Management, 29*(3), 333–349.

European Commission. (2021). *Industry 5.0: Towards a Sustainable, Human-Centric and Resilient European Industry*. Brussels.

Fortunato, M. W., Alter, T. R. (2011). The individual-institutional-opportunity nexus: an integrated framework for analyzing entrepreneurship development. *Entrepreneurship Research Journal, 1*(1), https://doi.org/10.2202/2157-5665.1002.

Gallo, I., Melé, D. (2025). Work integration of people with mental disorders through social enterprise: a humanistic-personalist framework and case study. *Journal of Business Ethics, 199*(4), 693–713.

Gregori, P. (2024). Entrepreneuring as provocation and its critical capacity: problemaizing and establishing meanings of entrepreneurship. *Entrepreneurship & Regional Development, 36*(9–10), 1188–1209.

Hardin, G. (1968). The tragedy of the commons: the population problem has no technical solution; it requires a fundamental extension in morality. *Science, 162*(3859), 1243–1248.

Harris, J. D., Sapienza, H. J., Bowie, N. E. (2009). Ethics and entrepreneurship. *Journal of Business Venturing, 24*(5), 407–418.

Illouz, E. (2007). *Cold Intimacies: The Making of Emotional Capitalism*. Polity Press, Cambridge.

Kahneman D. (1999). Objective happiness. In Kahneman, D, Diener E, Schwarz N, (Eds.), *Well-being: The Foundations of Hedonic Psychology* (pp. 3–25). Russell Sage Foundation, New York, NY.

Kirzner, I. M. (2009). The alert and creative entrepreneur: a clarification. *Small Business Economics, 32*, 145–152.

Krueger, N., Welpe, I. (2014). Neuroentrepreneurship: what can entrepreneurship learn from neuroscience. In M. H. Morris (Ed.), *Annals of Entrepreneurship Education and Pedagogy* (chapter 4, pp. 60–90). Edward Elgar Publishing, Cheltenham.

Krueger, N. F. Jr., Reilly, M. D., Carsrud, A. L. (2000). Competing models of entrepreneurial intentions. *Journal of Business Venturing, 15*(5–6), 411–432.

Kuratko, D. F., Morris, M. H., Schindehutte, M. (2015). Understanding the dynamics of entrepreneurship through framework approaches. *Small Business Economics, 45*(1), 1–13.

Linsley, P. M. (2017). Application of an ethics of care to business. In A. J. G. Sison, G. R. Beabout, I. Ferrero (Eds.), *Handbook of Virtue Ethics in Business and Management* (pp. 307–319). Springer, Dordrecht.

Marshall, A. (1890). *Principles of Economics*. Great Minds Series, London.

Massaro, S., Drover, W., Cerf, M., Hmieleski, K. M. (2023). Using functional neuroimaging to advance entrepreneurial cognition research. *Journal of Small Business Management, 61*(2), 938–966.

Matricano, D. (2023). Interdisciplinarity in Entrepreneurship: Investigating Issues and Debates with New Lenses. Springer Nature, Cham.

McEwen, B. S. (2004). Protection and damage from acute and chronic stress: allostasis and allostatic overload and relevance to the pathophysiology of psychiatric disorders. *Annals of the New York Academy of Sciences, 1032*(1), 1–7.

Mehta, P. H., Josephs, R. A. (2010). Testosterone and cortisol jointly regulate dominance: evidence for a dual-hormone hypothesis. *Hormones and Behavior*, *58*(5), 898–906.

Mehta, P. H., Welker, K. M., Zilioli, S., Carre, J. M. (2015). Testosterone and cortisol jointly modulate risk-taking. *Psychoneuroendocrinology*, *56*, 88–99.

Melé, D. (2024). *The Humanistic Person-Centered Company. Issues in Business Ethics* (Vol. 55). Springer, Cham.

Melo, H. L., Anderson, A. K. (2016). The function of positive emotions in exploration. In J. D. Greene, I. Morrison, M. E. P. Seligman (Eds.), *Positive Neuroscience* (pp. 209–233). Oxford University Press, Oxford.

Meng, H., Kim, J. (2025). Disability and entrepreneurial behavior: psychological barriers, knowledge and enablers. *Journal of Innovation & Knowledge*, *10*(5), 100794.

Miles, M. P., Munilla, L. S., Covin, J. G. (2004). Innovation, ethics, and entrepreneurship. *Journal of Business Ethics*, *54*, 97–101.

Mmbaga, N. A., Mathias, B. D., Williams, D. W., Cardon, M. S. (2020). A review of and future agenda for research on identity in entrepreneurship. *Journal of Business Venturing*, *35*(6), 106049.

Moroz, P. W., Hindle, K. (2012). Entrepreneurship as a process: toward harmonizing multiple perspectives. *Entrepreneurship Theory and Practice*, *36*(4), 781–818.

Munoz, P., Dimov, D. (2023). Facing the future through entrepreneurship theory: a prospective inquiry framework. *Journal of Business Venturing*, *38*(4), 106303.

Mzembe, A. N., Filimonau, V. (2024). No care without justice: a normative ethical perspective of the employment of people with disabilities in hospitality businesses. *Tourism Management Perspectives*, *51*, 101244.

Nicolaou, N., Shane, S. (2009). Can genetic factors influence the likelihood of engaging in entrepreneurial activity?. *Journal of Business Venturing*, *24*(1), 1–22.

Nicolaou, N., Shane, S. (2014). Biology, neuroscience, and entrepreneurship. *Journal of Management Inquiry*, *23*(1), 98–100.

Nicolaou, N., Shane, S., Cherkas, L., Spector, T. D. (2009). Opportunity recognition and the tendency to be an entrepreneur: a bivariate genetics perspective. *Organizational Behavior and Human Decision Processes*, *110*(2), 108–117.

Nofal, A., Nicolaou, N. (2021). The biology of entrepreneurship. In M. M. Gielnik, M. S. Cardon, M. Frese (Eds.), *The Psychology of Entrepreneurship* (pp. 60–79). Routledge, New York-London.

Nofal, A. M., Nicolaou, N., Symeonidou, N., Shane, S. (2018). Biology and management: A review, critique, and research agenda. *Journal of Management*, *44*(1), 7–31.

Passarelli, M. (2024). *L'Imprenditore Armonico. Un Approccio Multidisciplinare tra Etica e Benessere*. Rubettino, Soveria Mannelli, Catanzaro.

Passarelli, M., Bongiorno, G., Corrado, N. (2025). Social entrepreneurship education for university students: the experience of ENACTUS Italy. *The International Journal of Management Education*, *23*(3), 101239.

Radu-Lefebvre, M., Lefebvre, V., Crosina, E., Hytti, U. (2021). Entrepreneurial identity: A review and research agenda. *Entrepreneurship Theory and Practice*, *45*(6), 1550–1590.

Ranfagni, S., Runfola, A. (2018). Connecting passion: distinctive features from emerging entrepreneurial profiles. *Journal of Business Research*, *92*, 403–411.

Ricardo, D. (1817). *Principi di Economia Politica e dell'Imposta*. UTET, Torino.

Rodriguez, A. C., Ardichvili, A., Casa Nova, S. P. D. C., Quintão, A. A. (2025). Ethics of care in HRD practices: a case study of a Brazilian corporation. *European Journal of Training and Development*, https://doi.org/10.1108/EJTD-11-2024-0165.

Ryff, C. D., Singer, B. H. (2008). Know thyself and become what you are: A eudaimonic approach to psychological well-being. *Journal of Happiness Studies, 9*(1), 13–39.

Sanguedolce, M., Bongiorno, G., Passarelli, M., Catapano, G., Filice, L. (2025). Human wellbeing, societal needs and cutting-edge technology: a review on medical device technologies. *Technology Analysis & Strategic Management*, 1–17. https://doi.org/10.1080/09537325.2025.2545963.

Sarason, Y., Dean, T., Dillard, J. F. (2006). Entrepreneurship as the nexus of individual and opportunity: a structuration view. *Journal of Business Venturing*, *21*(3), 286–305.

Say, J.B. (1861), *Traite d'Economie Politique*. Calmann-Levy, Paris.

Schumpeter, J. A. (1934). *The Theory of Economic Development*. Harvard University Press, Cambridge.

Scheibel, O., Osiyevskyy, O., Radnejad, A. B. (2025). Strategic entrepreneurship in VUCA environment: the competing forces of outcome variability. *Management Research Review, 48*(2), 214–230.

Shane, S. (2000). Prior knowledge and the discovery of entrepreneurial opportunities. *Organization Science*, *11*(4), 448–469.

Shane, S. (2003). *A General Theory of Entrepreneurship: The Individual-Opportunity Nexus*. Edward Elgar, Cheltenham-Northampton.

Shane, S., Eckhardt, J. (2003). The individual-opportunity nexus. In Z. J. Acs, D. B. Audretsch (Eds.), *Handbook of Entrepreneurship Research: An Interdisciplinary Survey and Introduction* (pp. 161–191). Springer, Boston, MA.

Shane, S., Venkataraman, S. (2000). The promise of entrepreneurship as a field of research. *Academy of Management Review*, *25*(1), 217–226.

Shepherd, D. A., Patzelt, H. (2011). The new field of sustainable entrepreneurship: studying entrepreneurial action linking "what is to be sustained" with "what is to be developed". *Entrepreneurship Theory and Practice*, *35*(1), 137–163.

Shepherd, D. A., Patzelt, H. (2017). Trailblazing in entrepreneurship: Creating new paths for understanding the field. Springer Nature.

Shepherd, D. A., Williams, T. A., Patzelt, H. (2015). Thinking about entrepreneurial decision making: review and research agenda. *Journal of Management*, *41*(1), 11–46.

Smith, A. (1776). *The Wealth of Nations: An Inquiry into the Nature and Causes*. A cura di Edwin Cannan (1994), Modern Library/Random House, New York.

Stephan, U., Rauch, A., Hatak, I. (2023). Happy entrepreneurs? Everywhere? A meta-analysis of entrepreneurship and wellbeing. *Entrepreneurship Theory and Practice*, *47*(2), 553–593.

Steyaert, C. (2007). Entrepreneuring as a conceptual attractor? A review of process theories in 20 years of entrepreneurship studies. *Entrepreneurship and Regional Development*, *19*(6), 453–477.

Toledano, N. (2022). Restoring the Garden of Eden: a Ricoeurian view of the ethics of environmental entrepreneurship. *Business Ethics, the Environment e Responsibility*, *31*(4), 1174–1184.

Vallaster, C., Kraus, S., Lindahl, J. M. M., Nielsen, A. (2019). Ethics and entrepreneurship: A bibliometric study and literature review. *Journal of Business Research, 99*, 226–237.

Vlasov, M. (2021). In transition toward the egocentric entrepreneurship nexus: how nature helps entrepreneurs make ventures more regenerative over time. *Organization & Environment, 34*(4), 559–580.

Waldman, D. A., Wang, D., Fenters, D. (2016). Brain, biology, and context: an evolutionary perspective on entrepreneurship. *Journal of Business Venturing, 31*(5), 581–602.

Wang, C., Dai, M., Fang, Y., Liu, C. (2022). Ideas and methods of lean and agile startup in the VUCA Era. *International Entrepreneurship and Management Journal, 18*(4), 1527–1544.

Wiklund, J. (1999). The sustainability of the entrepreneurial orientation-performance relationship. *Entrepreneurship Theory and Practice, 24*(1), 37–48.

Wiklund, J., Nikolaev, B., Shir, N., Foo, M. D. (2017). Entrepreneurship and wellbeing: past, present, and future. *Journal of Business Venturing, 32*(3), 1–11.

Youssef, A. B., Boubaker, S., Omri, A. (2018). Entrepreneurship and sustainability: the need for innovative and institutional solutions. *Technological Forecasting and Social Change, 129*, 232–241.

5 The Humane, the *sapiens*, and the Harmonic Entrepreneurs

An explorative comparison and research agenda

Diego Matricano, Massimiliano Vesci and Mariacarmela Passarelli

5.1 The methodological approach

In the following sections, each of the three profiles discussed in this volume – the Humane, the *sapiens*, and the Harmonic Entrepreneur – is reconsidered. However, in this case, the analysis focuses not on the profile in question but rather on the three fundamental aspects that emerge from the profiles themselves. Their individual characteristics (which go beyond the traits analysed in the first chapter), the way they implement entrepreneurship processes, and the way they make decisions are analysed cross-sectionally to reveal how each profile relates to these fundamental aspects. The goal of this chapter is not to identify the best profile but to compare them and reveal how similar, or distant, these profiles are when they are entrepreneurial.

5.2 The Humane, the *sapiens*, and the Harmonic Entrepreneurs: are they different in terms of characteristics?

Previous Chapter 2 clarified that the concept of the Humane Entrepreneur is behavioural, embodying an entrepreneurial strategic posture characterized by three critical dimensions: Entrepreneurial Orientation (EO; Covin and Slevin, 1989), Sustainability Orientation (SO; Parente et al., 2021; Vesci et al., 2024), and Human Resource Orientation (HRO; Kim et al., 2018; Vesci et al., 2025) as delineated in prior research. Specifically, the Humane Entrepreneur is not characterized by specific traits, but it is typified through a strategic posture. This strategic posture or behaviour requests to act entrepreneurially, which means to play as an innovator, risk-taker, and in a proactive way. This behaviour cannot be symbolized as "humane" if it does not also exhibit significantly high levels of SO and HRO.

DOI: 10.4324/9781003681182-5

In Chapter 3, the characteristics of the *sapiens* entrepreneur (Matricano, 2024) have been identified in a posture based on wisdom and careful discernment. In this case, the notion of posture has been associated with the anatomical structure that implies to remain standing, reacting, and balancing the external forces in the context and assuming a good position to face market issues. Given that it is not only relevant to stand but also how to react and balance: wisdom and discernment represent the criteria the *sapiens* entrepreneur should use in their action.

Lastly, Chapter 4 evidenced that the Harmonic Entrepreneur (Passarelli, 2024) operates on the basis of three credos: (1) taking care for personal well-being; (2) taking care for people and common good; and (3) taking care of all the goods of the world and, more generally, of creation. In this sense, the Harmonic Entrepreneur adopts a lifestyle that decreases anxiety and stress, maintaining self-care, and develops the ability to set up human relationships across all life's domains. Accordingly, lifestyle and ability are the lens adopted to innovate, respecting environment and biodiversity, and to improve human well-being and dignity.

Starting from these premises, a comparison between the Humane, the *sapiens*, and the Harmonic Entrepreneurs shows that the basic characteristic of the Humane Entrepreneur is represented by the display of an entrepreneurial strategic posture. In this case, the posture is somewhat related to the strategic behaviour that must be primarily entrepreneurial. And entrepreneurial behaviour means a strategic behaviour at least devoted to innovation, to proactivity and to risk-taking (Covin & Slevin, 1989). The *sapiens* entrepreneur also has among its basic characteristics the display of a posture. On the contrary, in this case, the notion of posture is not related to the assumption of a certain type of strategic behaviour, but rather it regards a spatial and anatomical condition. This condition implies reactivity to contextual forces and balancing these forces to remain standing when facing market issues. The Harmonic Entrepreneur basically behaves by adopting a specific lifestyle (reducing anxiety and stress) and exercising specific abilities (that involve emotions). According to the above, the basic characteristics of the three entrepreneurial types are clearly different. The Humane Entrepreneur demonstrates a posture clearly rooted in entrepreneurship. In this sense, the basic characteristic of the Humane Entrepreneur has its reason why in entrepreneurship itself. Conversely, the *sapiens* and the Harmonic Entrepreneurs demonstrate a posture and a behaviour that are a sort of tool to exercise entrepreneurship, given that the *sapiens* posture, being anatomical and spatial, and the harmonic lifestyle, being emotionally based and relying on stress reduction, display clearly to be collateral to entrepreneurship: more in detail, the basic characteristics of the *sapiens* and the Harmonic Entrepreneur are preconditions to action.

Having acquired this point, what basic characteristics of the three entrepreneurs are specific and operating features that demonstrate? The Humane Entrepreneurs (1) have a necessary focus on orientation towards innovation, proactiveness, and risk-taking given that without it there is not any Humane Entrepreneur (i.e., EO feature), (2) take care of environment and society (i.e., SO feature), and (3) empower, empathize, and enable workforce for the betterment of their lifestyle (that is human-resource orientation feature). The *sapiens* entrepreneurs operationalize their posture through wisdom and discernment that are principles enabling judgement and action. Harmonic Entrepreneurs take care of their personal well-being (that is *Salus salutis* feature and credo), of people and common good (that is *Homo humanitas* feature and credo), and of good of the world and creation (that is *Homo humus* feature and credo). Comparing the operating features the three entrepreneurs demonstrate emerges that, although the Humane and Harmonic Entrepreneurs show different basic characteristics, they operationalize these characteristics in a very similar way (better, with similar features), searching for well-being of society, environment, and more in general people and business workforce. These characteristics imply that both types of entrepreneurs have specific strategic goals that enlarge entrepreneurial core domain. On the other hand, the *sapiens* entrepreneurs continue to demonstrate also with operating features preconditions to action or better the tools through which they behave. In this sense, operating features of the *sapiens* entrepreneur confirm that this entrepreneur's profile has characteristics that are positioned at a general level of action and not at a specific level (as the previous two profiles).

What are the implications of the aforementioned differences regarding profit interpretation and more in general enterprise's goals? Assuming the "meso-perspective" (Vesci et al., 2024, p. 95) in assessing firm performance, it is possible to go beyond the mere goal of financial profit expanding the purpose of the corporation (Cucino et al., 2025; Mayer, 2016, 2021), taking into account the well-being of human resources within the firm and its societal outcomes. Societal considerations include factors such as environmental stewardship, supplier relations, customer satisfaction, and broader interactions within the ecosystem in which the firm operates. Examining entrepreneurial behaviour through a meso-perspective, regarding both the Humane and Harmonic Entrepreneurs, at least three core dimensions for assessing performance emerge: care for the organization, care for people, and care for society. Caring for the organization involves ensuring its viability and preserving its social function. Addressing the needs of people – both employees and customers – fosters mutual commitment that facilitates the enhancement of EO capabilities. When innovation is pursued with strategic efforts to reduce environmental impact, minimize resource usage, and encourage sustainability, firms can cultivate societal commitment, which leads to long-term benefits. These benefits allow enterprises to create greater value for customers and implement strategies to support their workforce effectively (Vesci et al., 2025). In sum, within the context of performance assessments, we have a clear expansion of performance interpretation in the case of the Humane and Harmonic Entrepreneurs. The care for organization reflects firm's EO, including innovation, proactivity, and readiness for risk-taking (Covin & Slevin, 1989) and self-care personal well-being. The care for people emphasizes client satisfaction through value offerings while addressing employee needs by enabling "humane" and "harmonic" work conditions. This involves empowerment measures, engagement initiatives, and actions that promote employee enablement. Meanwhile, fostering sustainability demands strategic behaviours that encompass both environmental and social dimensions. To enhance social legitimacy, firms are strongly encouraged to adopt strategies that improve the quality of life within their local communities. These contentions demonstrate that for both Humane and Harmonic Entrepreneur profiles, these practices lead connaturally to clear outputs of performance evaluation under the meso-perspective approach, answering the call for an expansion of the purpose of the corporation required at the dawn of the twenty-first century (Business Roundtable, 2019; Cucino et al., 2025; Feola et al., 2025; Mayer, 2016, 2021). In the case of the *sapiens* entrepreneur, the expansion of the purpose of the business, and consequentially of firm performance assessment, is not a connatural and clear characteristic of the entrepreneurial profile (as in the Humane and Harmonic Entrepreneurs), but it is only a possibility. It means that the *sapiens* entrepreneur could expand business purpose beyond the mere financial goal but also could not. In addition, the purpose's expansion could possibly be directed differently from what the Humane and Harmonic Entrepreneurs do. Possibly, the expansion of the business purpose and its direction is directly related to the criteria (which and how) and the path adopted by entrepreneur in assuming *sapiens* decisions.

Differences and homogeneities among the three profiles of entrepreneurs that emerged from the above are displayed in Table 5.1.

5.3 The Humane, the *sapiens*, and the Harmonic Entrepreneurs: do they manage entrepreneurial processes in the same or different ways?

The profiles of the Humane, the *sapiens*, and the Harmonic Entrepreneur have emerged to fill the gap left by the utilitarian view of entrepreneurship, offering a model of the agent who, in response to complexity (VUCA) and societal demands, is able to balance profit with sustainability, care for human resources, ethical discernment, and the promotion of the common good.

The concept of the Humane Entrepreneur is grounded in Upper Echelons Theory (Hambrick and Mason 1984), which assumes that firms are the mirror image of their entrepreneurs and managers. Consequently, firms' strategic choices depend on the profile of their top managers and entrepreneurs. This has supported the shift from the firm level (of Humane Entrepreneurship, HumEnt) to the individual level. The *sapiens* entrepreneur's profile is conceived as an attempt to approach entrepreneurship studies from an interdisciplinary perspective, drawing on philosophy and classical studies, in particular

Table 5.1 A comparison between the Humane, the *sapiens*, and the Harmonic Entrepreneurs focused on their characteristics

Issue	The Humane Entrepreneur	The *sapiens* entrepreneur	The Harmonic Entrepreneur
Basic characteristics	Posture (entrepreneurial and strategic)	Posture (spatial and anatomical)	Lifestyle and abilities
Operating features	Caring for: entrepreneurship (entrepreneurial orientation, Covin & Slevin, 1989), environment and society (sustainability orientation, Parente et al., 2021); humane-resource (humane resource orientation, Kim et al., 2018)	Wisdom and careful discernment	Caring for: self-care and personal well-being, people and common good, good of the world and creation
Feature level	Specific	General	Specific
Final purpose and performance assessment	Clear (and directed) expansion	Expansion as a possibility	Clear (and directed) expansion

Source: Authors' personal elaboration.

the Senecan notion of Sapientia. The Harmonic Entrepreneur originates from the double nexus (individual-opportunity and individual-context), which recognizes that the entrepreneur co-evolves with opportunities and context, and is conceptualized as an agent of change at multiple levels, not only within their organizations but also within themselves. All the profiles are inspired by Covin and Slevin's thought (1991, p. 8): "A behavioural model of entrepreneurship is suggested because behaviours rather than attributes are what give meaning to entrepreneurial process". We know entrepreneurs through their actions. Entrepreneurs are seen as individuals who "exercise the power of transformative capacity" (McMullen et al., 2021, p. 1200) in a social system, deploying agency as an "ongoing activity" whereby they "reflect on and strategically operate within" the context(s) where they are embedded (Lawrence et al., 2011, p. 55).

Coherently, the defining feature of these three profiles, as opposed to earlier trait-based research, is their adoption of a dynamic, processual perspective (Gartner, 1988). This shift reframes the question from who possesses the right characteristics to how particular entrepreneurial profiles generate value through alignment between individual attributes and contextual conditions. The foundation for this comparison rests on the widely accepted definition of entrepreneurship as the study of how, by whom, and with what effects opportunities are discovered, evaluated, and exploited (Shane & Venkataraman, 2000). The analysis of the three profiles shows that they all engage with the same entrepreneurial process, from the individual entrepreneur's initial inspiration to opportunity exploitation, but they apply different ethical and strategic filters. Starting from the individual entrepreneur's initial inspiration, the *sapiens* entrepreneurs (Matricano, 2024) have a posture based on *sapientia*, combined with careful discernment. The core goal is to master human feelings (passions) with reason, and the greatness lies in the journey toward wisdom. This requires daily commitment, diligence in education, and self-control, looking for wisdom combined with careful discernment in judging and in operating. The Humane Entrepreneur's process is inspired by the individual's internal values and beliefs, which provide a visionary framework guiding the implementation of the core business idea (Parente et al., 2018). Specifically, in unfamiliar situations, the Human Entrepreneurs actively draw upon their intrinsic personal values and cultural background by enabling a scenario that takes into consideration environmental and local communities concerns as well as employees' empowerment and empathetic relationships. The combination of values and culture represented by entrepreneur's sensibility towards sustainability and human-resources concerns leads to the implementation and the exploitation of the core business idea initially conceived.

The Harmonic profile (Passarelli, 2024) is moved by the interaction of two main drivers: the quest to be well (personal well-being and flourishing) and to exist well (an entrepreneurship of care oriented towards others and the broader environment) (André & Pache, 2016). The concept of harmony serves as a guiding principle for inspiring entrepreneurs towards health, happiness, and social well-being.

How are their individual inspirations translated into opportunity evaluation? In the *sapiens* entrepreneur, evaluation is path dependence and previous experiences lock agents into or out of the possible options (Garud et al., 2010). For this profile, opportunities are evaluated through the pursuit for balance, striving to minimize negative conditions (pains) and maximize positive circumstances (gains) by balancing environmental, social, and economic aspects.

In the Humane Entrepreneurs, opportunity evaluation is based on Individual Humane Entrepreneurial Orientation (IHEO), which is an expanded strategic posture. IHEO requires high levels of traditional Entrepreneurial Orientation (EO) (innovativeness, risk-taking), Sustainability Orientation (SO), and Human-Resource Orientation (HRO). This integration ensures that the evaluation of financial goals is combined with broader objectives. The Harmonic Entrepreneur is someone who, in evaluating opportunities, integrates personal virtues and technical skills, long-term vision and executive discipline, attention to people, and respect for creation. The big challenge for the three proposed profiles is to advance a strategic vision of entrepreneurship that centres on the translation of ideas into concrete practices and outcomes (Mmbaga et al., 2020; Radu-Lefebvre et al., 2021).

For the *sapiens* entrepreneur, the exploitation of the opportunity aims at sustainable and broad-based objectives. The ultimate aim pursued is expected to go beyond personal and narrow goals, being reoriented towards social and widely shared objectives. Reason and ethics, which govern exploitation actions, can lead the *sapiens* entrepreneurs to shape stronger ventures, manage them more effectively, and make them last longer. The exploitation of an opportunity by the *sapiens* entrepreneur, in fact, is the act of transforming the idea into practice through the constant application of reason to balance contextual factors (the quest for balance), the continuous control of passions through reason, with the aim of creating value that is ethical, enduring, and aligned with wisdom. In fact, when reason and ethics take the place of passions, this can lead the *sapiens* entrepreneurs to shape stronger ventures, lead them more effectively, and make them last longer.

Therefore, for the *sapiens* entrepreneur, economic success (profit) is not the ultimate goal but rather an outcome that, when guided by wisdom and discernment, contributes to the strength and longevity of the venture, in the service of broader ethical and social objectives.

The exploitation of opportunities by the Humane Entrepreneur is manifested through the adoption of a visionary framework that shapes the implementation of the core business idea. The Humane Entrepreneur adopts an entrepreneurial strategic posture grounded in EO, but this posture is embedded within a broader value-laden and cultural context, reflected in the entrepreneur's sensitivity to sustainability and human-resources concerns. This combination of values and culture fosters an overarching visionary scenario that the Humane Entrepreneur subsequently leverages to effectively implement and exploit the initially conceived core business idea. In this sense, the act of implementation does not rely solely on innovation and financial risk-taking but on a value-rooted visionary framework that ensures business success is pursued coherently with care for key stakeholders (employees, local communities) and the natural environment (Parente et al., 2021; Vesci et al., 2024).

The Harmonic Entrepreneurs exploit opportunities by orchestrating knowledge, capital, and processes in a way that supports both performance and health (mens sana in corpore sano). They design routines of self-care (movement, exercise, rest, emotional regulation) and a work organization that reduces stress and burnout, fostering positive emotions, creativity, and passion for work. Exploitation is conceived as entrepreneurship of care, where the resources are mobilized to enable others to 'exist well'. The enterprise is seen as a communal entity, where customers receive fair value, collaborators reach an adequate standard of living, and communities benefit from responsible resource use. Moreover, the Harmonic Entrepreneurs exist well by acting for durable, purpose-aligned results (see Table 5.2).

Table 5.2 A comparison between the Humane, the *sapiens*, and the Harmonic Entrepreneurs regarding the processes they carry out

Stage	The Humane Entrepreneur	The *sapiens* entrepreneur	The Harmonic Entrepreneur
Individual inspiration for opportunity identification	Guided by internal values and beliefs, the entrepreneur adopts a visionary value-based frame for implementing the core business idea	Inspired by *sapientia* and discernment. Entrepreneur aims to master passions through reason and lifelong learning	Driven by the quest to *be well* and *exist well*, entrepreneur is led by harmony that guides the whole process (economic, health, social impact)
Opportunity evaluation	Entrepreneur evaluates opportunities through three main drivers: Entrepreneurship Orientation + Sustainability Orientation + Human-Resource Orientation, attempting to align profit and broader goals	Entrepreneur evaluates opportunities under path dependence, by seeking a balance of environmental, social, and economic gains vs. pains	Entrepreneur evaluates opportunities through harmony, by integrating virtues and skills, long-term vision, care for people, and respect for creation
Opportunity exploitation/ implementation	Opportunities are exploited via a value-rooted visionary framework. Profit is one of the outcomes that serves rather than replacing care for employees, communities, and environment	Opportunities exploitation has the aim to create ethical, durable value. Profit is conceived as an outcome that serves, rather than replaces, broader ethical and social aims	Opportunity exploitation has the goal to orchestrate resources. Profit is one of the outcomes that serve, rather than replace, personal well-being, harmony in the relations with stakeholders, and respect for the environment through responsible resource use

Source: Authors' personal elaboration.

The proposed analysis shows that the traditional entrepreneurial process remains structurally the same, for all the profiles, but the approach is different. The emergence of the profile approach (the Humane, the *sapiens*, and the Harmonic Entrepreneurs) signifies a critical paradigm shift. Entrepreneurship is seen as a process that develops and evolves over time and the focus shifts to 'entrepreneuring', defined as the act of acting, interacting, and constructing content through practices, processes, and contexts (Steyaert, 2007). Thus, entrepreneurial profiles represent a complex combination of personal attributes, experience, actions, context, and strategic choices. Moreover, the profiles show a new approach that turns the entrepreneurial process into a set of highly individualized strategic decisions influenced by deeply embedded values and contextual challenges. Thus, while the traditional entrepreneur exploits opportunities with a primary focus on profit, the Humane, the *sapiens*, and the Harmonic profiles conceive exploitation as the act of strategically orchestrating resources to sustain ethics and generate value that goes beyond financial returns, encompassing social and environmental benefits; additionally, by drawing on wisdom, provide a long-term orientation that supports the venture's robustness and enduring success.

In this view, the entrepreneurial process encompasses opportunity recognition, evaluation, and exploitation, from the entrepreneur's initial inspiration to the implementation of the business idea.

5.4 The Humane, the *sapiens*, and the Harmonic Entrepreneurs: are they different in the way they make decisions?

To compare the decision-making processes implemented by each profile, it is necessary to start from the specific definitions offered before.

As argued in Chapter 2, the genesis of the Humane Entrepreneurs' decision-making appears to be fundamentally rooted in the personal values and cultural background of the entrepreneurs themselves (Parente et al., 2021; Vesci et al., 2024, 2025). Specifically, this combination of values and culture – represented by entrepreneur's sensibility towards sustainability and humane-resources concerns – seems to foster a visionary framework or scenario. This overarching vision is subsequently adopted by the Humane Entrepreneurs, who leverage it to effectively implement and exploit the core business idea that was initially conceived. Thus, familiarity or unfamiliarity with the situation plays a clear role in moving the decision-making towards adoption.

In Chapter 3, it is argued that the *sapiens* entrepreneurs (Matricano, 2024) can master their passions through reason and express personal coherence. They are committed to continuous improvement, living a daily ethical path oriented toward wisdom. According to this perspective, entrepreneurship processes (Matricano, 2025a, 2025b) and related decisions are helpful for entrepreneurs to put into practice daily commitment, diligence in education, and self-control inspired by *sapientia*, i.e., by reason that governs the passions.

Eventually, in Chapter 4, it is shared the idea that the Harmonic Entrepreneur – someone who integrates personal virtues and technical skills, long-term vision and executive discipline, attention to people, and respect for creation while recognizing, evaluating, and realizing opportunities – reveals a distinctive approach to entrepreneurial decision-making, one that deliberately harmonizes profit with well-being and the common good (Passarelli, 2024). In this view, harmony becomes a guiding design and evaluation principle throughout the entire entrepreneurial process (opportunity discovery, evaluation, and exploitation) within a co-evolving nexus among individuals, opportunities, and contexts. Thus, entrepreneurship returns to being what it can and must be: a practice of responsible freedom that creates a future on a human scale.

At this state, the comparison among the Humane, the *sapiens*, and the Harmonic Entrepreneurs can be conducted. For a start, attention needs to be paid on the premises that determine the decisional process and the results they aim to achieve. The Humane Entrepreneurs rely on personal values and cultural background, and they express their sensibility towards sustainability and humane-resources concerns in their decisional process. The *sapiens* entrepreneurs place reason before passions. They do not refer to specific or idiosyncratic conditions, but they orient their decisions on a daily ethical path oriented toward wisdom, tending to continuous improvement. The Harmonic Entrepreneurs rely on personal virtues and technical skills and aspire to responsible freedom that creates a future on a human scale. According to the above, the roots of decision-making clearly differ. In fact, the Humane Entrepreneurs rely on personal characteristics to make decisions that can have a positive impact for the society. The *sapiens* entrepreneurs refer to general values in order to have a social impact and – in turn – improve themselves. The Harmonic Entrepreneurs rely on both personal characteristics and specific (technical) knowledge to positively impact the society. What is the achieved result? Decision-making processes are developed along different paths.

The Humane and Harmonic Entrepreneurs move from an individual to a social level. They make their own abilities available to others to generate a shared positive impact. The *sapiens* entrepreneurs, instead, start with a social level (ethics and wisdom), act at a social level (they make decisions to create a shared positive impact) but – in the end – they take advantage of their choices to improve themselves as well. Decisions are made and evaluated to get themselves closer to ethics and wisdom. While the *sapiens* entrepreneurs' decision-making reveals retroaction (the *sapiens* entrepreneurs are inspired by ethics and wisdom and this generates a positive impact for the society as a whole and for themselves specifically), the Humane and Harmonic Entrepreneurs do not reveal this so clearly. Actually, by going through the profiles of the Humane and the Harmonic Entrepreneurs, it is reasonable to argue that they can revise and fine-tune their characteristics after each choice, but in these cases, there is no predetermined personal goal to achieve. For the *sapiens* entrepreneurs, instead, the personal goal to achieve is clear since the beginning and all the efforts are made to get closer to it.

What does the above differences imply? The main implication that can be drawn from the above-mentioned differences concerns the implementation of

Table 5.3 A comparison between the Humane, the *sapiens*, and the Harmonic Entrepreneurs concerning their decision-making processes

Issue	The Humane Entrepreneur	The *sapiens* entrepreneur	The Harmonic Entrepreneur
Basics	Personal values and cultural background	Reason that governs the passions	Personal virtues and technical skills
Paths	From an individual to a social level	From a social level to a social and individual level	From an individual to a social level
Individual characteristics	Are revised and fine-tuned after each choice	Are developed according to ethics and wisdom	Are revised and fine-tuned after each choice
Perspective	Instrumental	Additive	Instrumental
Implementation	Realistic	Challenging	Realistic

Source: Authors' personal elaboration.

decisions. All the profiles look at the future, but while the Humane and the Harmonic Entrepreneurs think and act according to an additive perspective, the *sapiens* entrepreneurs do it according to an instrumental perspective. Whether or not they predetermine a personal goal to achieve influences the decision-making processes and differentiates them. For the Humane and the Harmonic Entrepreneurs, every decision is autonomous and is made to maximize impact at that time, in that context. They can learn something new after making a decision (as mentioned, it is reasonable to argue that they can revise and fine-tune their characteristics after each choice, but in these cases, there is no predetermined personal goal to achieve). For the *sapiens* entrepreneurs, instead, every decision is part of a chain that tends to maximize the impact and personal growth in the light of a predetermined goal.

That said, it is important to emphasize that the decision-making process is designed to be implemented. The reference to an additive or instrumental perspective requires evaluating the feasibility of these decision-making paths. While the additive decision-making processes implemented by the Humane and the Harmonic Entrepreneurs are more realistic (decisions are made in this time, in this context), the instrumental decision-making processes implemented by the *sapiens* entrepreneurs are more challenging (considering the long-term generated impact, there is a risk of sacrificing short- to medium-term impact).

A summary of the differences emerging from the above is included in Table 5.3.

5.5 Final remarks and research agenda

The comparison among the Humane, the *sapiens*, and the Harmonic Entrepreneurs is not intended to determine the best, most complete, or effective profile. Rather, it is conducted in an attempt to remark an ongoing shift in entrepreneurship studies (specific traits do not seem to meet the expectations of scholars and practitioners and are therefore being replaced by profiles, composed of several traits or better characteristics) and to raise new questions and, potentially, open new streams of research (Matricano 2023).

First, scholars in the field of entrepreneurship are encouraged to validate or reject the shift from traits to profiles. Does it make sense to consider entrepreneurs from a broader perspective? Can profiles help conduct research about entrepreneurs in a more effective way?

Second, what areas of research depend on entrepreneurial profiles? In this volume, entrepreneurial profiles – based on certain characteristics – are correlated with entrepreneurial processes and decision-making. The phases and activities they implement and the way they make their decisions seem to depend on the profile. Naturally, other areas of research can be suggested and evaluated.

Third, are the profiles presented in this volume representative of entrepreneurs? Are there other profiles that could be presented to enrich the analysis? The Human, the *sapiens*, and the Harmonic Entrepreneurs are defined according to previous studies and research. Thus, other characteristics could be added to these profiles or – realistically – other profiles could be presented.

Overall, the description of the Humane, the *sapiens*, and the Harmonic Entrepreneurs is not intended to be definitive. On the contrary, it is hoped that these profiles will attract the attention of other scholars and fuel a debate that deserves considerable attention to advance entrepreneurship studies.

References

André, K., Pache, A. C. (2016). From caring entrepreneur to caring enterprise: addressing the ethical challenges of scaling up social enterprises. *Journal of Business Ethics*, 133(4), 659–675.

Business Roundtable. (2019). Statement on the purpose of a corporation. Available at: https://opportunity.businessroundtable.org/wp-content/uploads/2019/12/BRT-Statement-on-the-Purpose-of-a-Corporation-with-Signatures.pdf.

Covin, J. G., Slevin, D. P. (1989). Strategic management of small firms in hostile and benign environments. *Strategic Management Journal*, 10(1), 75–87.

Covin, J. G., Slevin, D. P. (1991). A conceptual model of entrepreneurship as firm behavior. *Entrepreneurship Theory and Practice*, 16(1), 7–25.

Cucino, V., Feola, R., Ferlito, R., Maiolini, R., Michelini, L., Mongelli, L., Pavlovic, A., Piccaluga, A., Rullani, F., Tafuro, M., Vesci, M. (2025). What do we really mean by "purpose-driven businesses"? *Sinergie Italian Journal of Management*, 43(1), 21–45.

Feola, R., Michelini, L., Piccaluga, A., Pirson, M., Brunetti, F. (2025). Imagining a better world: how are companies transforming capitalism? *Sinergie Italian Journal of Management*, 43(1), 11–17.

Gartner, W. B. (1988). "Who is an entrepreneur?" is the wrong question. *American Journal of Small Business*, 12(4), 11–32.

Garud, R., Kumaraswamy, A., Karnøe, P. (2010). Path dependence or path creation? *Journal of Management Studies*, 47(4), 760–774.

Hambrick, D. C., Mason, P. A. (1984). Upper echelons: the organization as a reflection of its top managers. *The Academy of Management Review, 9*(2), 193–206.

Kim, K. C., El Tarabishy, A., Bae, Z. T. (2018). Humane entrepreneurship: how focusing on people can drive a new era of wealth and quality job creation in a sustainable world. *Journal of Small Business Management, 56*(S1), 10–29.

Lawrence, T., Suddaby, R., Leca, B. (2011). Institutional work: Refocusing institutional studies of organization. *Journal of Management Inquiry, 20*(1), 52–58.

Matricano, D. (2023). *Interdisciplinarity in Entrepreneurship. Investigating Issues and Debates with New Lenses*. Springer Nature, Cham.

Matricano, D. (2024). Entrepreneurship: shaping the future | the manifesto. *International Entrepreneruship and Management Journal*, 20(4), 3113–3123.

Matricano, D. (2025a). Dynamic capabilities in entrepreneurship – DyCE: a new domain for theoretical and empirical research. *Journal of Small Business Management*. https://doi.org/10.1080/00472778.2025.2503372.

Matricano, D. (2025b). Dynamic capabilities in entrepreneurship. In J. Mitra (Ed.), *The Palgrave Encyclopedia of Entrepreneurship* (pp. 1–5). Palgrave Macmillan, Cham.

Mayer, C. (2021). The future of the corporation and the economics of purpose. *Journal of Management Studies, 58*(3), 887–901.

Mayer, C. (2016). Reinventing the corporation. *Journal of the British Academy*, (4), 53–72.

McMullen, J. S., Brownell, K. M., Adams, J. (2021). What makes an entrepreneurship study entrepreneurial? Toward a unified theory of entrepreneurial agency. *Entrepreneurship Theory and Practice, 45*(5), 1197–1238.

Mmbaga, N. A., Mathias, B. D., Williams, D. W., Cardon, M. S. (2020). A review of and future agenda for research on identity in entrepreneurship. *Journal of Business Venturing*, 35(6), 106049.

Parente, R., El Tarabishy, A., Botti, A., Vesci, M., Feola, R. (2021). Humane entrepreneurship: some steps in the development of a measurement scale. *Journal of Small Business Management*, 59(3), 509–533. https://doi.org/10.1080/00472778.2020.1717292.

Parente, R., ElTarabishy, A., Vesci, M., Botti, A. (2018). The epistemology of humane entrepreneurship: theory and proposal for future research agenda. *Journal of Small Business Management*, 56(S1), 30–52.

Passarelli, M. (2024). *L'Imprenditore Armonico. Un Approccio Multidisciplinare tra Etica e Benessere*. Rubettino, Soveria Mannelli.

Radu-Lefebvre, M., Lefebvre, V., Crosina, E., Hytti, U. (2021). Entrepreneurial identity: a review and research agenda. *Entrepreneurship Theory and Practice*, 45(6), 1550–1590.

Shane, S., Venkataraman, S. (2000). The promise of entrepreneurship as a field of research. *Academy of Management Review*, 25(1), 217–226.

Steyaert, C. (2007). 'Entrepreneuring' as a conceptual attractor? A review of process theories in 20 years of entrepreneurship studies. *Entrepreneurship and Regional Development*, 19(6), 453–477.

Vesci, M., Botti, A., Parente, R. (2024). The Humane Entrepreneurship framework. In A. Botti, R. Parente (Eds.), *Humane Entrepreneurship and Innovation* (Emerald

Studies in Sustainable Innovation Management) (pp. 89–103). Emerald Publishing Limited, Leeds. https://doi.org/10.1108/978-1-83797-374-320241006.

Vesci, M., Feola, R., Parente, R., Botti, A. (2025). Does humane entrepreneurship have value? Exploring the link between employees' beliefs and firm financial performance: a perceptual approach. *International Entrepreneurship and Management Journal*. https://doi.org/10.1007/s11365-025-01151-z.

Index

For Product Safety Concerns and Information please contact our
EU representative GPSR@taylorandfrancis.com Taylor & Francis
Verlag GmbH, Kaufingerstraße 24, 80331 München, Germany